Mastering
Scrapbook
PAGE DESIGN

with Michele Gerbrandt

design secrets made simple

MEMORY MAKERS BOOKS

Executive Editor Kerry Arquette *Founder* Michele Gerbrandt

Senior Editor Lydia Rueger

Art Director Nick Nyffeler

Graphic Designers Robin Rozum, Andrea Zocchi

Art Acquisitions Editor Janetta Abucejo Wieneke

Craft Editor Jodi Amidei

Photographer Ken Trujillo

Contributing Photographers Brenda Martinez, Jennifer Reeves

Contributing Writers Heather A. Eades, Elizabeth Shaffer Harlan, Heidi Schueller

Editorial Support Karen Cain, Emily Curry Hitchingham, MaryJo Regier, Dena Twinem

Contributing Memory Makers Masters Valerie Barton, Joanna Bolick, Jennifer Bourgeault, Christine Brown, Susan Cyrus, Kathy Fesmire, Brandi Ginn, Diana Graham, Angie Head, Jeniece Higgins, Diana Hudson, Torrey Miller, Kelli Noto, Michelle Pesce, Shannon Taylor, Denise Tucker, Andrea Lyn Vetten-Marley, Samantha Walker, Sharon Whitehead, Holle Wiktorek

Memory Makers® Mastering Page Design With Michele Gerbrandt

Published by Memory Makers Books, an imprint of F+W Publications, Inc.

12365 Huron Street, Suite 500, Denver, CO 80234

Phone (800) 254-9124

First edition. Printed in the United States.

08 07 06 05 04 5 4 3 2 1

Library of Congress Cataloging-in-Publication Data

Gerbrandt, Michele
   Mastering scrapbook page design : design secrets made simple / with Michele
Gerbrandt.-- 1st ed.
     p. cm.
   Includes bibliographical references and index.
   ISBN 1-892127-37-7
   1. Photographs--Conservation and restoration. 2. Photograph albums. 3. Scrapbooks. I.
Title: Scrapbook page design. II. Title

TR465.GA799 2004
745.593--dc22

                                                       2004060984

Distributed to trade and art markets by

F+W Publications, Inc.

4700 East Galbraith Road, Cincinnati, OH 45236

Phone (800) 289-0963

ISBN 1-892127-37-7

Memory Makers Books is the home of *Memory Makers*, the scrapbook magazine dedicated to educating and inspiring scrapbookers. To subscribe, or for more information, call (800) 366-6465.
Visit us on the Internet at www.memorymakersmagazine.com.

This book belongs to

_____

Table of contents

Chapter 1: Understanding Color 12-35

Chapter 2: Learning Layout 36-57

charme de village

THE GRACEFUL FLOW OF METAL FENCE . . .

THE BEAUTY OF A SCULPTED POST . . .

HOW JOURNEY OPENS UP YOUR EYES

TO THINGS UNNOTICED OTHERWISE!

Introduction

In 12 years as part of the scrapbook industry, I've seen a lot of fantastic layouts. As a former graphic designer myself, I'm amazed at how many scrapbookers instinctively create layouts using the principles I studied in college! When I compliment scrapbookers' great color choices or keen sense of design, they are quick to respond with things like "I don't have any design training" or "It just looked good to me—I'm not really sure why."

In *Mastering Scrapbook Page Design With Michele Gerbrandt*, you'll learn how to make certain design choices based on basic principles of design. After all, the goal of professional graphic designers is to communicate a concept or idea visually, and the same is true for scrapbookers. Whether you'd like to express the excitement and energy of winning the big game or the love you feel toward your newborn child, your layout, colors, embellishments, title treatment and journaling should work together to communicate your experiences for future generations. You become "designers" of your photos and personal stories.

For beginners, these concepts will serve as a strong foundation for creating visually appealing layouts with confidence every time. For more advanced scrapbookers, they'll affirm what you might have been doing all along. Throughout the chapters Understanding Color, Learning Layout, Creating Balance and Adding Finesse, you'll discover 13 secrets to successful design that I've learned over the years. In addition, a section on finding design inspiration in everyday places and a complete glossary of design terms makes this book a must-have resource for every scrapbooker. Once you learn the rules of design, you'll begin to discover when it's OK to break them. And that's the most exciting part!

Michele

Michele Gerbrandt
Founding Editor
Memory Makers magazine

Get Inspired by Your Environment

Looking for fresh ideas for designing great pages? Your environment can serve as layout inspiration in more ways than you might have imagined, whether you are indoors or out. Consider the color combinations and patterns in the wings of a butterfly, the dramatic shapes and lines present in mountain peaks or the shades of sunset on a clear night. Any of these natural wonders can be re-created from paper, paints and other supplies to form interesting page backgrounds, borders or embellishments. Likewise, more design ideas can be gleaned from the fonts used on product packaging, the design of a picture frame, a piece of clothing or any other item. The following examples show how scrapbookers have incorporated bits of their surroundings on pages. See the list on page 10 for other places you can look when stuck for fun and innovative page inspiration.

At first glance, these items may not look like they have much in common, but they can all be inspiration for scrapbook pages. Watch your surroundings for interesting patterns, color combinations and shapes that could be used in page design.

Adapt a Jewelry Design

Jodi designed a heritage frame that was inspired by an old necklace. Although the shape and style of the heritage frame is different from the necklace, Jodi incorporated the idea of a hanging gemstone by suspending a small slide mount inside a larger one with eyelets.

Jodi Amidei, Memory Makers Books

Supplies: Fabric patterned paper (K & Company); slide mounts and bottle cap (Design Originals); ribbon (Offray); clear lacquer (Plaid); eyelets; metal ring

Utilize Office Supplies

Binder rings from the office supply store inspired the border on Antuanette's page. She printed images of a shoreline, cut them to fit inside the rings and attached them to her page. She continued the circular metallic theme by setting eyelets down each side of one photograph.

Antuanette Wheeler, Winter Garden, Florida

Supplies: Blue papers; eyelets; fibers; binder rings; seaweed stamp (source unknown); stamping ink; silver embossing powder

Use a Fabric Pattern

Pennie designed a page of her college-bound daughter to match an old piece of fabric. For the background, she punched circles from black paper and vellum, arranged so they overlapped and placed tiny punched shapes of tan vellum in the open spaces. She carried the fabric's circle pattern over to her title by pairing smaller vellum pieces with letter stickers.

Pennie Stutzman, Broomfield, Colorado

Supplies: Patterned vellums (Paper Company, Treehouse Designs, Kangaroo and Joey); letter stickers (EK Success); college mascot die cut (Sports Solution); buttons (Jesse James); silver glitter pen (American Crafts); punches (Emagination Crafts, Family Treasures); light green and yellow cardstocks; vellums; ribbon

Find Everyday Inspiration in:

Amusement parks	Flags	Menus	Purses
Architecture	Floor tile	Money	Road signs
Billboards	Gardens	Needlework patterns	Sale brochures
Bricks and stones	Gift wrap	Newspaper personal ads	Shadows
Calendars	Graffiti	Packaging	Sheet music
CD cases	Hand mirrors	Paper towels	Shoes and footprints
Children's books	Holiday decorations	Pasta	Solar system
Coats of arms	Inside the refrigerator	Perfume bottles	Toy stores
Computer	Instruments	Pet food	Universal symbols
Credit cards	Jewelry	Picture frames	Vases
Dishes	Junk mail	Postage stamps	Video games
Fabric	Leaves	Posters	

Copy a Blueprint

Kelly created lettering for this page that resembles the style on a blueprint. In addition, she copied and trimmed pieces of the blueprint to use as page accents.

Kelly Angard, Highlands Ranch, Colorado

Supplies: Tan patterned paper (Carolee's Creations); mesh (Magenta); blue, brown and off-white cardstocks; nails; washers; blue pen

Be Inspired by Nature

Polly was inspired by the delicate simplicity of nature for this tag. She first covered the tag with patterned paper, and then adhered a silk leaf to the underside. She attached an eyelet through both tag and leaf, and fastened the ribbon in place. After decorating and adhering the frame to the tag, she added a flower with a button to accentuate the design.

Polly McMillan, Bullhead City, Arizona

Supplies: Patterned paper and stamps (PSX Design); silk leaf and flower (Wal-Mart); metal frame and sticker (K & Company); ribbon (Offray); button (Making Memories); eyelet (Creative Imaginations); vellum

Chapter 1

Understanding Color

Color adds life to your scrapbook pages. It can enhance your photos, tie a layout together or create a mood to support the story behind the page. Color also helps identify holidays, seasons, objects and even gender—red and green are associated with Christmas, brown and orange reflect autumn, pink is traditionally for girls and blue for boys. Scrapbook supplies are often organized by color, proving once again how important it is for page design.

In this chapter, you'll learn the rules of contrast, how to properly combine colors and patterns and how to use a color wheel. These concepts will help you develop a deeper understanding of color and allow you to use it effectively on your layouts.

Caroline

Choose a triadic color scheme

Lively shades of violet, green and orange make the perfect triadic color scheme for Shannon's page, as based on the color wheel. Shannon inked her patterned papers to create definition around the edges. She painted the metal letters, brads and flowers to further coordinate with her color scheme.

Shannon Taylor, Bristol, Tennessee

Supplies: Floral patterned paper (Anna Griffin); green textured paper (Artistic Scrapper); metal flowers and letter stamp (Making Memories); metal letters (Creative Imaginations, Making Memories); stamps (Hero Arts); ribbon (Offray); mulberry cardstock; stamping inks; brads; acrylic paints

Design secret #1: *Contrast*

Learning to apply proper contrast is simple (that's why it's first in this book) and can instantly improve the look of your page. Before choosing background papers to go with your photos, ask yourself whether your photos are dark or light in value. If your photos are light-toned, place them on a dark background, and if they are dark, choose a lighter background. A contrasting background will allow the edges of your photos to be more defined, thus keeping the focus on the photos. While the basic idea of contrast is best illustrated in black and white, the same light/dark concept holds true when using color photos and color backgrounds.

Seeing Love in Black and White

Place light photos on a dark background

BEFORE: On white cardstock, there is little contrast between the edges of the light-toned photos and the background. The edges of the photos are barely visible in some places.

BEFORE & AFTER

AFTER: When the same photos are placed on a black background, there is a bold contrast between the two. The photos stand out nicely and the edges are well-defined.

Lydia Rueger, Memory Makers Books

Supplies: Metal letters and accents (Scrapyard 329); white and black cardstocks; white and black pens; black acrylic paint

Baseball

Mat a photo in a contrasting shade

A light-colored mat around a sepia-toned photo helps make it a pop-fly, right off the page! Here, Kathy used a variety of dark-valued papers for her background to create a winning contrast with the photo. She used walnut ink to saturate various elements on the page, such as the stencil and wooden tags, and smudged the torn edges of her papers for even more contrast.

Kathy Fesmire, Athens, Tennessee

Supplies: Patterned paper (K & Company); tan brick-patterned paper (Sandylion); baseball phrase stickers (Karen Foster Design); letter stamps (PSX Design); wooden letters (Laura's Crafts); walnut ink (Postmodern Design); leather string (www.thedesignerslibrary.com); lettering template (source unknown); tags (Pebbles); envelope (American Tag); cream, brown and gray cardstocks; ribbons; black stamping ink

Cute Cowgirl

Play up heritage photos on a contrasting background

Memories don't have to fade away when they get a kick of life from a page that plays up contrasting values. These black-and-white photos with white borders draw in the eye when set against dark brown patterned papers. The dark title letters on a light strip of paper and journaling tag matted on dark brown echo this contrasting effect.

Valerie Barton, Flowood, Mississippi
Photos: Elwyn Gray, Jackson, Mississippi

Supplies: Patterned papers and patterned slide mount (Design Originals); cream textured cardstock (National Cardstock); letter stickers, definitions and labels (Pebbles); star punch (McGill); star brads (Making Memories); tag template (Deluxe Designs); clear photo corners (Fiskars); dark brown cardstock; transparency

It's War At Last

Use contrasting shades to focus on memorabilia

Holle highlights some of her husband's military awards by mounting the light-colored documents on a dark background. Holle scanned, reduced and printed copies of the certificates, then adhered them to brown cardstock she had cut into a file folder shape. Behind the awards, foreign currency and photocopies of newspapers stand at attention against the black inked edges of the layout. The contrasting shades keep the page balanced, while gold embossed words coordinate with metallic military embellishments.

Holle Wiktorek, Reunion, Colorado
Photo: Thomas Wiktorek, Reunion, Colorado

Supplies: Gold embossing powder; letter stamps (La Pluma); dog tag and chain (Li'l Davis Designs); military medallion charms (K & Company); kraft, dark brown and black cardstocks; foam tape; black stamping ink; paper clips

Cruising Cuisine

Highlight memorabilia in a clear pocket

To keep the focus on her memorabilia, Pamela mounted the generally light-colored menus on a dark green background, inside a pocket made from a clear page protector. To set her journaling apart from the menus, Pamela printed it on cream paper, then double matted it with dark green and silver. Silver square tiles and metallic lettering create a feeling of industrial elegance, while also contrasting well against the dark background.

Pamela James, Ventura, California

Supplies: Metallic patterned papers, wire mesh and scale embellishment (Club Scrap); epoxy stickers (Creative Imaginations); metal letters (Making Memories); dark green cardstock; silver pen; page protector; brads; green thread

Beautiful Girls

Select light patterned papers for dark photos

BEFORE: On top of a deep floral pattern, these photos seem to get lost in the shadows. The mostly dark photos blend into the page background.

TIP: If you're not sure whether certain color photos read light or dark, copy them in black-and-white on a copy machine before choosing page colors. If your copies have medium gray value, then either a dark or light background will work.

AFTER: Here, the same photos are given life when mounted on contrasting petal-soft springtime shades. The simple, daisy-patterned paper complements the content of the photos while allowing them to pop off the page.

Angie Head, Friendswood, Texas

Supplies: Patterned papers, address labels, rivets and nails (Chatterbox); ribbons, flowers, label holders, brads and metal-rimmed tags (Making Memories); letter stamps (EK Success, Hero Arts); tiny glass marbles; black pen; acrylic paint; stamping inks

Puppy Love
Break the rules of contrast

Once you've learned the rule of contrast, you'll learn that sometimes it's OK to break it. Even though Angie's photos have black backgrounds, it works to mount them on dark cardstock because the subjects are so bright. In fact, the black-on-black design makes the subjects appear silhouetted—they stand out even more than if they were on a light background. In addition, the white journaling strips in the center of the page create a sharp contrast to the background and coordinate with the subjects.

Angie Head, Friendswood, Texas

Supplies: Patterned paper (7 Gypsies); red mesh (Magic Mesh); ribbon, metal letters, safety pin and page pebbles (Making Memories); bottle cap (Li'l Davis Designs); title letters (Chatterbox); black cardstock; button; white and red cardstocks; foam tape; eyelets; acrylic paint

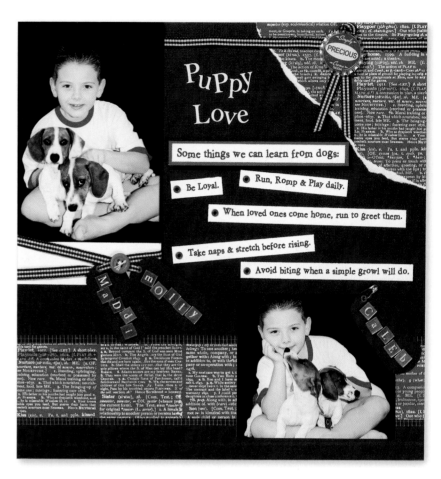

Basketball
Mat light- and dark-valued photos differently

How do you get two opposite-valued photos to pop with equal intensity? Here, Kelli mounted a lighter focal-point photo onto black cardstock for contrast. The darker secondary photo was mounted onto cream-colored cardstock, creating contrast while unifying the layout's color scheme.

Kelli Noto, Centennial, Colorado

Supplies: Patterned paper (My Own Design, MOD); letter and square die cuts (QuickKutz); pumpkin, vanilla, black and cream cardstocks; transparency

Matting Ideas

Keep the rules of contrast in mind when matting photos, then have fun with the variety of techniques and products shown here.

Michelle Pendleton, Colorado Springs, Colorado

Adam's Retreat

A light denim frame accented with brown ink creates a down-to-earth accent for a playful photo.

Supplies: Chalk ink (Clearsnap); leather strips (Prym-Dritz); tag (Creative Impressions); star charms and rub-on letters (Making Memories); jump rings (Westrim); round rub-on letters (Creative Imaginations); denim fabric; black pen

First Birthday

A photo of a baby bathed in pink frosting lends itself to monochromatic pink embellishing. Torn edges revealing a darker shade for contrast, as do a row of playful star brads.

Supplies: Star brads (Happy Hammer); lettering template (Crafters' Workshop); pink cardstocks

Luke

A blue mat draws out the color of the boy's shirt. Applying white modeling paste over crimped cardstock adds contrast as well as an interesting texture.

Supplies: Paper crimper (Marvy); modeling paste (Liquitex); letter stamps and jump ring (Making Memories); tag (Creative Impressions); twine; watermark and solvent inks; tan, blue and sand cardstocks

Kyle

Torn patterned paper and hand-stitching help to set visually stimulating boundaries. Thin blue mats give this child's eyes an extra spark.

Supplies: Blue and orange textured cardstocks (Bazzill); patterned paper (Carolee's Creations); letter conchos (Colorbök); embroidery floss; watermark ink

Design secret #2: Color Theory and Combinations

Even though you learned in elementary school that yellow and blue make green, it can be more difficult to understand how color theory applies to creating scrapbook pages. While scrapbooking doesn't usually involve mixing colors to make new ones, selecting multiple colors to make harmonious combinations on pages is where the color wheel can help. Understanding the organization of the wheel and seeing how complementary, analogous and other combos are derived will help you determine which colors best accent your photos. And when it comes to choosing colors for page backgrounds, photo mats and other embellishments, you can combine with confidence, knowing the theory behind your choices.

Family Ties

Use primary colors

Siblings beam from these black-and-white photos accented with the three primary colors. Red tags and polka-dot ribbons tie in to the background. Torn blue cardstock behind the photos creates a bold contrast with vibrant yellow patterned paper, buttons and heart accents. By using balanced amounts of each color, the red, yellow and blue create a harmonious color relationship.

Polly McMillan, Bullhead City, Arizona

Supplies: Yellow polka-dot papers (Lasting Impressions); gingham ribbon (Queen & Co.); postage charm and metal label holder (www.maudeandmillie.com); polka-dot ribbon (Offray); heart punch (EK Success); buttons (Making Memories); label maker (Dymo); letter stamps (PSX Design); black stamping ink; letter beads; red, blue and white cardstocks

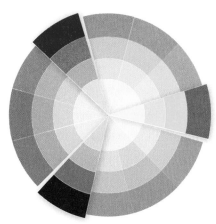

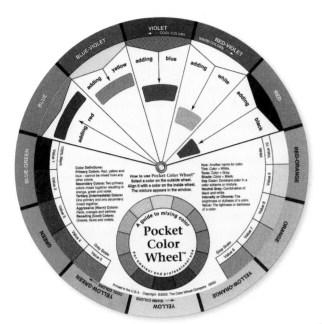

Defining and Combining Colors

Good color choices are the foundation of a successful scrapbook page. The color wheel makes it easy to choose great combos for pages each time. Look for color wheels at art and craft stores, and you'll discover that many include color-combining reference information right on the wheel so you never have to guess about what goes well together.

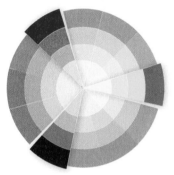

Primary colors

Red, yellow and blue. No other colors can be mixed together to create these colors.

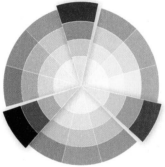

Triadic complements

Three colors equally spaced from each other on the colors wheel. Their placement on the wheel forms a triangle.

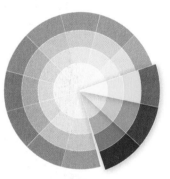

Analogous colors

Colors located next to each other on the color wheel. Because these colors are similar, they go together well.

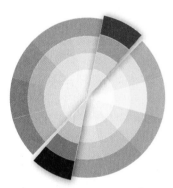

Complementary colors

Colors that are located directly across from one another on the color wheel.

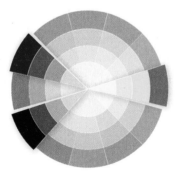

Split complements

A color that is paired with the two colors located on either side of its complement.

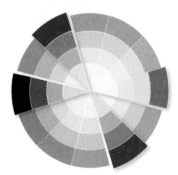

Double complements

Pairs of complementary colors used together.

More Combinations

Secondary colors: Purple, green and orange. Colors derived by combining primaries (red + blue = purple, yellow + blue = green, yellow + red = orange).

Monochromatic colors: Various shades, tints or tones of one color.

Tertiary colors: A primary color mixed with a secondary color.

Achromatic colors: A colorless scheme comprised of blacks, whites and grays.

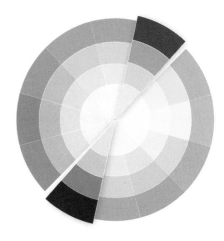

Goofy Guy

Select complementary colors in varying shades

Often, color combinations that work well on clothing also work for scrapbook page design. The stripes of this boy's shirt inspired Vicki's color scheme. She used various shades and patterns of two complementary colors—blue and orange—for everything from mimicking the exact pattern of the shirt on a tag to photo mats and journaling blocks.

Vicki Harvey, Champlin, Minnesota

Supplies: Patterned paper (Provo Craft); "Chase" letter stickers (Chatterbox); "Guy" and "2" stickers (Doodlebug Design); date stamp, metal letter charms and metal corners accents (Making Memories); label tape (Dymo); natural, navy blue, light blue and burnt orange cardstocks; black stamping ink, metal-rimmed tags; brads

Friendships Bloom in the Spring

Accent with analogous colors

Pretty shades located next to one another on the color wheel make Shelley's springtime photos come to life. Multiple cardstocks and patterned papers in green and yellow harmonize with dainty embellishments, photos and green journaling.

Shelley Paton, Morgan Hill, California

Supplies: Yellow-green and green patterned papers (NRN Designs); yellow patterned papers (K & Company); daisy eyelets (Got Memories); fibers and metal-rimmed tag (Making Memories); 3-D daisy stickers (EK Success); wire; beads; metal charms (Westrim); white, yellow and green cardstocks; vellum

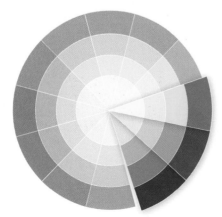

Haley Underground
Choose a triadic color scheme

Dark-toned photos of a field trip come alive when combined with a vibrant triadic color scheme—colors that are equally spaced on the color wheel to form a triangle. Torrey cut strips of red-orange, yellow-green and blue-violet to match colors in the photos, then wove the strips together, using blue-violet as the dominant color, red-orange as the subordinate and lime green to accent. Beams of bold color pull the eye across the page.

Torrey Miller, Thornton, Colorado

Supplies: Metal ball chain, metal letter tags and metal-rimmed tags (Making Memories); black chalk ink (Clearsnap); date stamp; white, blue-violet, red-orange and lime green cardstocks; foam spacers

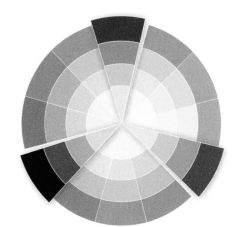

> *TIP:* Choose colors for pages that are appropriate to the emotion you wish to capture. Reds, oranges and yellows are considered warm and aggressive colors, while greens, blues and violets are cool and receding colors.

A Gift of Sunshine
Match color values

BEFORE: The yellow ribbon and evergreen photo mats are more saturated colors than the pastel lavender flowers, ribbons, and soft purple embossed paper. The colors chosen for the page match, but they have different values.

BEFORE & AFTER

TIP: Unless you are using a mono-chromatic color scheme, its a good idea to pair colors with similar values. For example, soft pink would work better with sage green than neon green.

AFTER: Light yellow ribbon and sage green photo mats complement the lavender flowers, embossed paper and background paper much better. The tone of the page is soft and subtle instead of conflicting.

Andrea Lyn Vetten-Marley, Aurora, Colorado
Photos: Lifetouch/JC Penney, Aurora, Colorado

Supplies: Lavender embossed paper (Hobby Lobby); patterned paper (EK Success); flower embellishment (Hirschberg Schutz & Co.); ribbon (Offray); ribbon corners (Creative Imaginations); thread; purple, sage green and cream papers

Uncharted Territory

Include monochromatic shades

Dana captured playfulness and femininity by selecting different shades of one color to produce a monochromatic color scheme. Pink patterned papers in a range of light to dark values create depth. Pink ribbon, similar to that in the subject's hair, pulls together her range of pink tones nicely. Tiny flower tacks carry through the flower motif for a page that's as fun as getting into Mommy's makeup.

Dana Smith, Eden Prairie, Minnesota

Supplies: Patterned papers, patterned vellum and flower tacks (Chatterbox); circle punch (Creative Memories); rub-on title lettering, metal-rimmed tag and ribbon (Making Memories); letter epoxy sticker (Creative Imaginations)

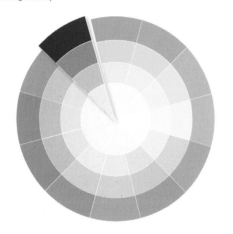

Create Yourself

Choose an achromatic scheme

For a classic design that captures the dignity of a black belt, Jlyne used a colorless scheme of blacks, whites and grays known as achromatic. Dark gray patterned paper frames black-and-white photos with formality and wisdom. While the photo on the upper right-hand side is actually in color, its subtle shades match the colorless design. Black brads, ink and gingham ribbon contrast with the bright white areas for a unified layout that really packs a punch.

Jlyne Hanback, Biloxi, Mississippi

Supplies: Dark gray patterned paper (7 Gypsies); rub-ons and black brads (Making Memories); gingham ribbon; white cardstock; black stamping ink

J'aime Paris à Printemps

Combine a color with a neutral tone

Beth brings a trendy yet sophisticated style to a black-and-white photo by pairing it with pink with black. When combined with a color, neutral black appears to deepen the color's value and makes the color pop.

Beth Akins, Louisville, Kentucky

Supplies: Patterned and pink papers (KI Memories); lip sticker (Treehouse Designs); patterned vellum (NRN Designs); letter beads; square pewter brads (Making Memories); circle clips (Target); black and white cardstocks; gingham ribbon; wire; black slide holder; foam spacers; fibers; envelope

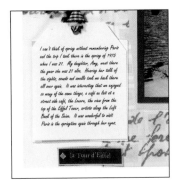

TIP: When unsure what to combine with a single bright color, try black. It looks great with almost anything.

Cruisin' Together

Pair a neutral tone with a color for a pleasing combination

Neutral brown cardstock and a premade frame match well with bright blue to create a feeling of tranquility. Lindsay created the sand-and-sea feel by applying walnut ink to her cardstock and then crumpling the patterned paper to offer the feel of ocean waves. The blues and browns complement the sky, sea and skin tones found in the photographs. Blue buttons, mesh and inked edges unify the page.

Lindsay Teague, Phoenix, Arizona

Supplies: Patterned paper (K & Company); premade frame (Cropper Hopper); pebble letters, phrase sticker, letter tile stickers, rub-on words, ribbon and staples (Making Memories); embossed "&" sticker (Creative Imaginations); letter cut-outs (Foofala); paper clips; fabric word tag (Me & My Big Ideas); gold circle clip (7 Gypsies); blue mesh (Magic Mesh); buttons (Making Memories, SEI); brown cardstock; walnut ink; blue stamping ink; gold floss; black slide mount; black pen

Choosing Color Combos for Photos

The most carefully chosen color scheme won't work well on a scrapbook page if it does not coordinate with the colors in your photographs. The examples here illustrate good color combinations that also bring out the best in Michele Gerbrandt's photos. In addition, when using a large quantity of one color, it's often a good rule of thumb to use smaller amounts of coordinating hues.

TIP: A color wheel that includes small windows like the one shown right allows you to frame your photos with various color schemes in order to choose the best dominant color.

Design secret #3: Patterns

Combinations of patterns are everywhere in home décor, from the kitchen wallpaper and border to the bedroom duvet and sheets. Myriad patterned papers are available as well, making it a staple supply for scrapbookers. As your stash of patterned paper grows, you'll want to get the most out of them on your pages. There are some rules that will make combining patterns easier, especially if you are venturing away from solids for the first time. 1. Always mix a big pattern with a smaller pattern. Two bright papers with large flowers will compete with one another for attention, but a bright flower pattern paired with a subtle pinstripe will go together nicely. 2. In most cases, it is a good idea to use more of the small pattern than the big one as to not detract from your photos. 3. Combine a light pattern with a dark pattern. If you're not sure if your patterns "read" light or dark, squinting can help. In addition, many companies make paper lines that contain a variety of monochromatic or coordinating patterns that were designed to work well together.

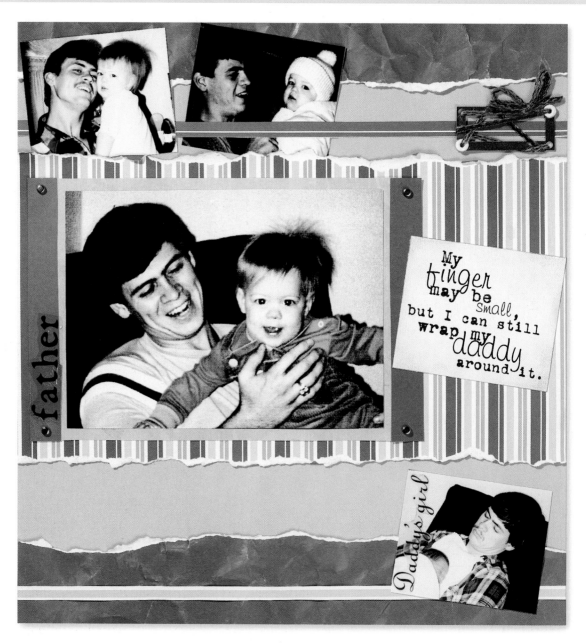

Father

Mix a pattern with a solid color

Sometimes one patterned paper design paired with coordinating solid colors is all you need for a cohesive layout. When pairing a pattern with a solid, you eliminate the hassle of trying to combine multiple patterns properly—just choose a solid color from the pattern and combine them. A soothing background of sage paper stabilizes the photos on this page beneath bold stripes. Strips of purple and two thin strips cut from patterned paper coordinate easily with the simple stripe without overpowering it.

Alicia Schubert, Mooresville, Indiana
Photos: Dawn Schubert, Mooresville, Indiana

Supplies: Striped, sage and purple papers (Colorbök); vellum word and phrase (DieCuts with a View); metal label holder and brads (Making Memories); eyelets; fibers; sage and purple papers

Precious

Pair multiple patterns in coordinating colors

Using muted colors to harmonize with the neutral photos, Carrie combined several different patterns in the same colors. Choosing patterns from the same company line made paper selection easy. A large block pattern works well with the smaller grid design, as well as with the thinner stripe. Carrie coordinated her patterns further by inking each one. Blue stitched frames allow her photos to stand out among the many patterns.

Carrie Zohn, Monroe, North Carolina

Supplies: Patterned papers and vellums (Chatterbox); indigo epoxy stickers (Creative Imaginations); silver heart (Jesse James); date stamp (Office Max); "Precious" rub-on (Making Memories); label maker (Dymo); stamping ink

Pinwheel

Combine patterns with same values

A color's level of brightness or dullness is known as its value or intensity. When combining patterned papers, keep their values in mind. All three patterns on Mary Anne's page are deep jewel tones. The papers' similar values make them go together well. The flower embellishments, in similarly valued metallics, add shine to the deep-toned background.

Mary Anne Walters, Ramsdell, Hampshire, England

Supplies: Magenta, green and purple patterned papers (Wordsworth); flower stickers (Herma); purple and black cardstocks; foam tape; chalk; black stamping ink

Fall

Mix faux finishes

The natural artistry of autumn is captured on this page by mixing a variety of faux finished patterns. Heather combined equal amounts of light and dark patterns for balance. The left side mimics earth-toned crumbled paper, while the right captures the essence of trees with a light-valued bark pattern. A rustic premade frame and square door image coordinate with the background. Heather continues the faux finish theme by adding printouts of letters from old signs, taken on her digital camera.

Heather Hadley, Orem, Utah

Supplies: Olive patterned paper (EK Success); cream patterned paper (Karen Foster Design); faux wood frame and door accents (My Mind's Eye); patterned vellum (source unknown); cardstock; brads; foam tape

TIP: Apply the same rules of color combination when adding fabric or other embellishments to pages. If you wouldn't select forest green paper, for example, to accent a predominantly pale pink page, then dark green ribbon wouldn't be the best choice either.

Ants

Combine monochromatic patterns and accents

Tara combined warm and rustic patterns to capture her daughter's discovery of ants. Striped and map patterned papers in sepia tones are interesting but not overpowering to her detailed black-and-white photos. Rickrack in a similar shade, along with typed journaling and letter stickers, add detail to the monochromatic color scheme.

Tara Pollard-Pakosta, Libertyville, Illinois
Photos: Ellen Bartlett, Libertyville, Illinois

Supplies: Striped paper (K & Company); map patterned paper (source unknown); rickrack ribbon (Me & My Big Ideas); staples; rivets (Prym-Dritz); letter stickers (Chatterbox); rust and tan cardstocks

Audrey
Capture elegance with similarly styled patterns

Large flower and flowing script patterned papers give grace and unity to this bright-eyed baby's special page. Holly combined these two separate patterns with the same elegant feel, melding them together by applying chalk and walnut ink to the torn edges. The powder-pink title and the satin green ribbon provide a polished look to the page, in fashionable Hepburn style, drawing from the patterned paper hues. The frilly sticker frame in the lower left corner gives this page its final piece of finesse.

Holly VanDyne, Mansfield, Ohio
Photo: Angie Rayburn, Picture Perfect Studios, Mansfield, Ohio

Supplies: Patterned papers and sticker (K & Company); walnut ink (7 Gypsies); ribbon (Anna Griffin); ribbon charm (Making Memories); plastic letters (source unknown); letter stamps (PSX Design); pink papers; black stamping ink; chalk

3
Combine multiple patterns with playful styles

Cheerful and bubbly, this page giggles by itself through the use of bright and playful patterns. Becky used equal amounts of the two patterns, trimming them on an angle for visual fun. The monochromatic yellow flower pattern plays well with the vibrant blue design that contains splashes of the same yellow. Although the two are from different companies, the combo provides an aesthetic playground for the simple black-and-white photo.

Becky Thompson, Fruitland, Idaho

Supplies: Blue patterned paper (Paper Fever); yellow patterned paper, colored circles number sticker and blue patterned square (KI Memories); metal-rimmed tags (Avery, Making Memories); square punch (Marvy); vellum; turquoise and white cardstocks

Tiny Flowers

Mix patterns with the same base color

BEFORE: While the pink designs in the light-yellow patterned paper match the pink page embellishments, the yellow base color does not coordinate as well as it could with the white-based patterned background paper. One's eye is drawn to the block of yellow instead of to the photograph and the interesting lettering details.

BEFORE & AFTER

AFTER: Using a white-based pattern that matches the background softens the impact across the page's center. The black-and-white photo remains the feature attraction, and the lettering details stand out more.

Shelley Rankin, Fredericton, New Brunswick, Canada

Supplies: Black textured papers (Sweetwater); brick patterned paper (Paper Loft); yellow patterned paper (Making Memories); white patterned paper (source unknown); flowers, brads, ribbon, photo corners (Making Memories); letter stickers (EK Success, Wordsworth); metal tag; pink cardstock; transparency; buttons; stencil; black stamping ink

Bon Voyage
Use smaller amounts of larger patterns

Muted, subtle plaid and map patterned papers make up the majority of the background of this heritage page. To add color, Andrea tore small pieces from a larger rose pattern, inked the edges and used them as accents. Had she chosen the rose pattern for her entire background, the bright magentas and greens would take the focus away from the page's most important elements—the photo, journaling and memorabilia.

Andrea Lyn Vetten-Marley, Aurora, Colorado

Supplies: Patterned papers (Chatterbox, Karen Foster Design, Making Memories); clock embellishments (7 Gypsies); seal embellishment (K & Company); ribbon charm, brads and safety pins (Making Memories); chalk stamping inks (Clearsnap); extra thick embossing powder; forest green and cream cardstocks; memorabilia; thread; clasp; ribbon; embossing ink; buttons; pen tip

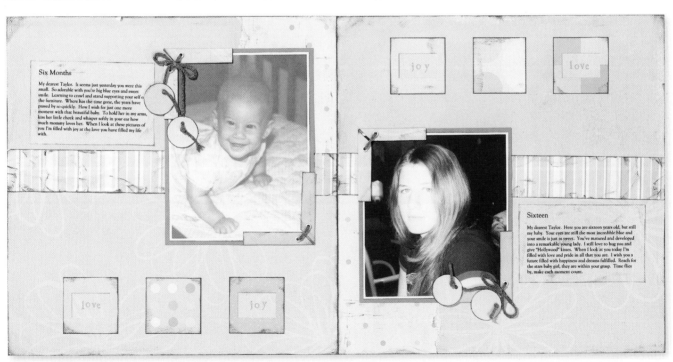

Six Months
Let a subtle pattern form your background

Dar used large blocks of sage patterned paper on either side of this spread. The monochromatic design is subtle enough to use in large quantities and not detract from other page elements. Smaller portions of polka dots and stripes unify the spread and serve as complements to the subtle pattern.

Dar Kaso, Virginia Beach, Virginia

Supplies: Patterned and pink papers, frames and cut-outs (KI Memories); fibers (Fiber Scraps); letter stamps (PSX Design); eyelets; brown and gray stamping inks; vellum; sandpaper

Chapter

2

Learning Layout

For graphic designers working on posters, magazine spreads, company logos and other projects, a good design communicates a message, organizes information and attracts the eye. These same goals of good design can be applied when working with photos, memorabilia and embellishments to create scrapbook pages. Each page element should work together to tell the page's story so it is cohesive, easy to understand and enjoyable to view.

The principles of using grids, shape, space and focal point as they relate to layout are discussed in this chapter in order to help you create a basis for successful pages every time.

On the day we brought John home from hospital, you instantly went from baby to big girl in my mind. I couldn't even believe how BIG you looked compared to tiny John. He is so lucky to have you you'll be a great big sister. ♥ Mommy

Little Girl, Big Sister

Balance a vertical photo with a horizontal pattern

Jeniece enlarged one photo to use as her focal point, and balanced the vertical photo with a wide, horizontal pattern across the bottom. Her title's position adds flow and movement to the page, while crumpled paper, burlap and metal embellishments add playful texture.

Jeniece Higgins, Lake Forest, Illinois

Supplies: Patterned papers (Daisy D's, Rusty Pickle); pigment paint (AMACO); letter charms and metal corner accents (Provo Craft); rub-on word, letter stamps, metal border strip and safety pin (Making Memories); wood letters (Li'l Davis Designs); pink and blue papers; notebook paper; burlap; rose stamping ink

Design secret #4: *Grids*

When you look at design in magazines, on posters or even on packaging, often that layout was built on a grid. Grids break a square or rectangular space into smaller, equal segments. This gives designers a framework on which to work and serves as a placement guide for text and images. A grid structure can also help when building scrapbook pages. One way is to divide a page into thirds, both vertically and horizontally. When the smaller squares made by the dividing lines are grouped to form different combinations, a variety of layout options is possible. All the pages in this section were designed using the same grid of thirds—the individual elements are just arranged differently.

The Team

Build a spread on a basic grid

A simple three-column grid was used as the framework for both sides of this spread. The right page is divided into equal thirds, while on the left side, the title comprises two-thirds of the page. Celine offered equal weight to both sides by typing "Team" in a larger point size and embellishing it with wooden posts and pieces of raffia to tie everything together.

Celine Hidalgo, Montreal, Quebec, Canada

Supplies: Patterned paper (C-Thru Ruler); mini eyelets (Making Memories); herb punch (EK Success); cream cardstock; raffia; brown pen; colored pencils

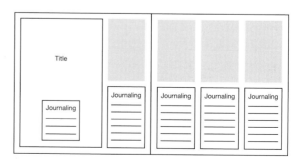

Fall

Organize page elements on a grid

BEFORE: While all elements on the page work well together, it's their placement that leaves the eye hanging. All the weight sits heavily in the lower left corner due to lack of grid division, pulling the eye away from what should be the focal-point photo.

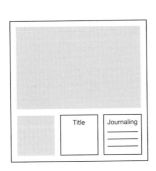

The colors of fall are so beautiful. I took these pictures on the Boulder Valley Farms property where our friends live. Fall and spring are my favorite times of year because it's when everything is changing and the colors are always breathtaking.
October 2003

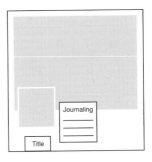

AFTER: By spacing out the lower elements into three distinct sections, the layout falls right into place. A title framed with a green slide mount in the bottom center of the page carries the eye straight down the path in the photo.

Brandi Ginn, Lafayette, Colorado

Supplies: Patterned papers (Karen Foster Design); circle clips (Creative Impressions); fibers (EK Success); slide mount (DMD); script stamp (Hero Arts); brown and black stamping inks; transparency; white and orange cardstocks; buttons

Sweet Silly Faces

Divide a page into nine equal squares

Up, down and all around, this layout models standard use of a grid. Brandi divided this page into thirds horizontally and vertically, breaking up the space equally into nine smaller, equal sections. Each square has interest all its own through the use of metal-rimmed tags, fibers, title letters and the painted transparency journaling block. By layering patterned papers at an angle across the background, Brandi softened the linear appearance of the page, reflecting the playful side of her daughters.

Brandi Ginn, Lafayette, Colorado

Supplies: Patterned papers (Chatterbox); fibers (EK Success); metal-rimmed tags (Avery); jump rings (Junkitz); Letter die cuts (QuickKutz); letters stamps (Foofala); acrylic paint; black pen

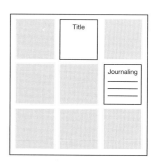

TIP: Using the same grid layout on every page of a mini theme album will allow you to finish the project more quickly and provide consistency throughout.

Friends

Combine small squares with rectangles

Here, Brandi strongly emphasized the vertical thirds of the layout through the use of smaller squares on the right. Her horizontal title and 4 x 6" photos make up the other two-thirds of the page. Circle patterned paper adds interests through the use of another shape.

Brandi Ginn, Lafayette, Colorado

Supplies: Circle patterned paper and preprinted title (Pixie Press); green and blue/gray papers; brads

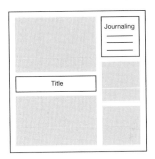

Botanical Gardens

Break a grid into many different sizes

Brandi varied the three-column grid by incorporating tiny squares, one large square and several different-sized rectangles for a page that flows horizontally. Small journaling strips are arranged vertically, then placed on a photo mat to maintain the consistency of the grid. Chalked edges help to unify page elements.

Brandi Ginn, Lafayette, Colorado

Supplies: Fish, flower and square punches (EK Success); yellow, blue, green, orange and cream cardstocks; chalk

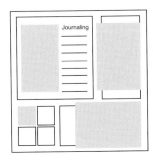

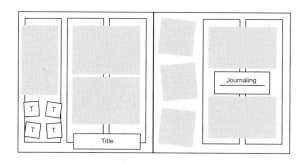

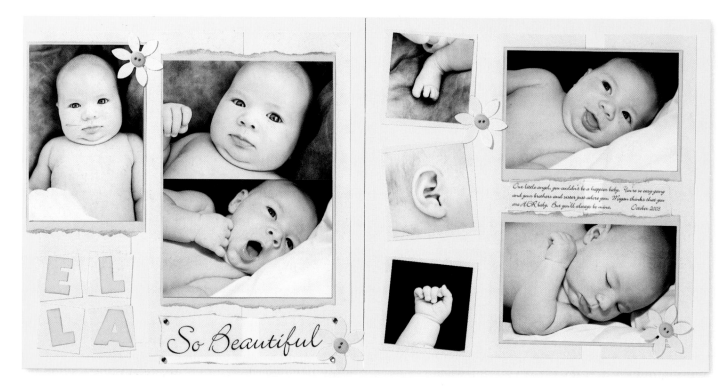

Ella

Layer horizontal photos on a vertical background

While babies bring such joyful chaos to ordinary lives, images in arrangements of three give order to this spread of baby Ella. The three rows of pink on each page immediately organize the page vertically. The blue title squares in the lower left corner break up the vertical arrangement, as do the horizontal 4 x 6" photos that extend over two pink columns on both sides.

Brandi Ginn, Lafayette, Colorado

Supplies: Flower punch (EK Success); letter die cuts (Sizzix); yellow, pink and blue cardstocks; buttons, chalk; vellum; brads

The Rule of Thirds

The concept of dividing a space into equal thirds is also a helpful method for a basic rule of photography. The Rule of Thirds, as it is known, divides a space into nine equal sections with vertical and horizontal lines. For a pleasing composition, your subject should fall on or near any of the points where the lines intersect. While this rule isn't the be all and end-all of photo composition, it's almost always a good option when in doubt of how to frame a certain shot.

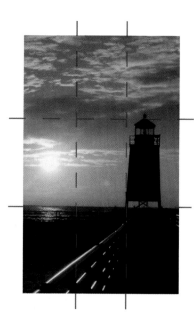

In Love

Create focal point with horizontal photos

Horizontal photos matted together that stretch across two thirds of the page define the page's focal point. Filling the remainder of the grid, a vertical photo and journaling block balance the horizontal photos.

Brandi Ginn, Lafayette, Colorado

Supplies: Letter die cuts (Sizzix); letter stamps (Hero Arts); red, blue and orange cardstocks; tag; fibers; photo corners; black stamping ink

Adam and his new girlfriend Kathryn came to visit. They met at school and have only been dating a couple of months. However, my mom tells me they spend every waking hour together. Something that is very unusual for Adam to do. We'll just have to see what happens.

in LOVE

We went camping with my mom and dad and the boys. Noah was enthralled with the firewe had to keep a close eye on him. He loved to watch the flames and hold on to the stick roasting marshmallows. Logan helped out just like a good big brother should. It was so relaxing to be outside in the fresh air. 6/98

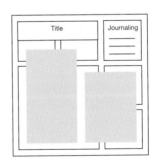

Carefree Campers

Offset photos on a vertical grid

By using darker green rectangles over a light green background, Brandi immediately establishes order and structure for her page. While the color blocks themselves make up a vertical grid, the photos were placed between the columns for a more interesting arrangement.

Brandi Ginn, Lafayette, Colorado

Supplies: Preprinted title (Pixie Press); letter stamps (Hero Arts); rust, cream, light and dark green papers; fibers; button; tag; orange stamping ink

Design secret #5: Shape and Line

When used properly, shapes can help communicate the messages of your layouts and support concepts. For example, photographs from a day at the ocean could be complemented with papers cut into wavy strips and layered across the background. While layering straight strips of paper across the background would look fine, the shapes present in the waves better communicate the idea of being at the ocean. Shapes can also help draw attention to a photo or image. Cropping a photo into a circle, for example, could focus in on the face of a person for an "All About Me" page while eliminating distracting or unnecessary background elements. Experiment with shape when cropping photographs, creating embellishments and placing journaling.

TIP: When cropping photos to place more focus on an image or fit within a certain layout, be careful not to crop too tight. You might lose interesting foreground or background details, or the subject will be left without breathing room.

Diamond Head

Crop photos into fitting shapes

The diamond shape of the center photo reinforces the page theme, as well as draws the eye into the scenic view. By cropping other photos into smaller diamond shapes and incorporating them into the design, Jen was able to incorporate personal touches while keeping the focus on the center photograph. Arranging the title in opposing diagonals supports the diamond shape, as does the torn paper background that mimics mountain peaks and waves.

Jen Lowe, Lafayette, Colorado

Supplies: Modeling paste (Liquitex); tonal applicator (A Stamp In The Hand); four-leaf clover punch (Punch Bunch); brown, blue, pink, yellow and green cardstocks; vellum; stamping inks; beads; foam tape

Twin Brothers

Utilize the positive and negative space of shapes

Letters are made up of shapes too, and can serve as design elements as well as sources of information. Here, Michelle utilized positive and negative space by cutting out title letters with a craft knife from gold and blue papers, using computer fonts as a guide. She played up shapes on this layout by enlarging the starting letters of her title words and allowing the sharp angles of the "t" and rounded curve of the "b" to extend off the main title block. She included smaller letters cut using templates to support the idea of using positive and negative space.

Michelle Pendleton, Colorado Springs. Colorado

Supplies: Blue and gold textured cardstocks (Bazzill); lettering template (Crafter's Workshop); watermark ink; black pen; embroidery floss

Wishes

Contrast sizes of page elements

When placed side by side, big and small page elements become more impactful. The large, horizontal rectangle of the focal-point photo is balanced by a smaller vertical rectangle photo in a decorative frame. The rectangular theme is repeated throughout with the fabric blocks, envelope, tags and title.

Diane Graham, Barrington, Illinois

Supplies: Fabric (Junkitz); die-cut title, hat die cut and tag template (Deluxe Designs); ribbon, flower, brads, staples, definition tags, photo corners and label holder (Making Memories); frame (K & Company); stick pin and paper clip (EK Success); fabric word sticker (Mrs. Grossman's); pink cardstock; chalk; walnut ink

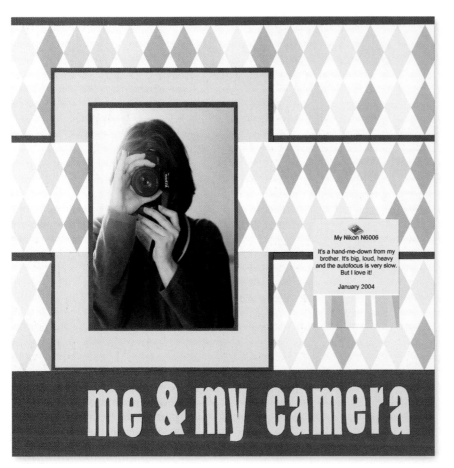

Me & My Camera
Design with shapes that support page theme

BEFORE: While these colors work well together and the layout is clean, the diamond shapes in the patterned paper do not relate to the page theme, and distract from its focus. The eye is pulled away from rather than drawn to the photo (specifically the camera lens), due to the motion created by the shapes.

BEFORE & AFTER

AFTER: This deluge of circles supports the concept of a round camera lens. The echoing circles help keep the camera as the focus rather than the hands that hold it. The circular theme is continued in the title letters and journaling.

Tracy Miller, Fallston, Maryland

Supplies: Patterned papers and tag (SEI); concho (Scrapworks); circle accents (KI Memories); rub-on word (Making Memories): foam tape; brown and blue cardstocks

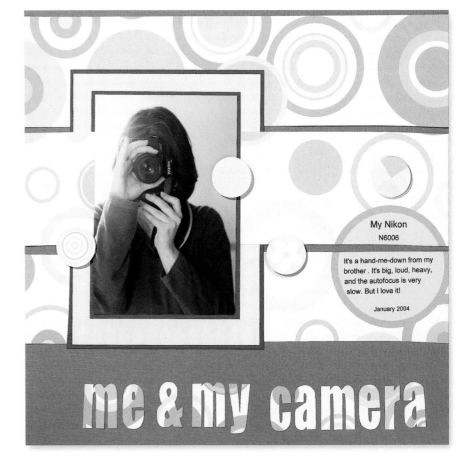

Super Star

Crop photos to complement page concept

BEFORE: Detail photographs of the subject's costume were cropped into small rectangles and matted on cardstock decorated with glitter. While small cropped photos add interest to the design, their shape does not complement the page concept.

AFTER: The same detail photos were cropped into star shapes to tie in with the page title, "Super Star." In addition, the use of another shape adds a touch of playfulness to the page, which fits well with both a child's recital and the whimsical computer font chosen for journaling.

Kimberly Lund, Wichita, Kansas

Supplies: Letter cut-outs (Hot Off The Press); glitter (Magic Scraps); star template (Provo Craft); brown and copper cardstocks

Three Types of Shapes

Think about the items in your home or your yard. Everything around you has a shape of some kind. Since scrapbook pages are typically comprised of squares and rectangles, incorporating unique and uncommon shapes on a page immediately draws attention. Designers break shapes of our world into three categories. 1. Geometric shapes: circles, squares, rectangles, triangles, etc. Geometrics are structured and make up the basis of scrapbook pages. 2. Natural shapes: plants, animals and people. Incorporating natural shapes on scrapbook pages can create a serene and fluid feel. 3. Abstract shapes: simplified versions of natural shapes, such as the symbols designating men's and women's restrooms. Using these can give your pages a unique, contemporary look.

The focal point of your scrapbook page is the first place your eye is drawn to when you look at a layout. Without a focal point, your eye doesn't know where to go and the layout could seem confusing. Most often a page's focal point is a bright, well-composed photograph, but if your photos of a certain event didn't turn out as well as you planned, draw attention to your title, journaling or embellishments that support the page theme. The first step is to choose what you'd like to emphasize. Was your child's favorite part of the amusement park the ice cream-cone she ate? Enlarge a photo of her enjoying her treat to serve as your page's focal point. Focal point can also be created through matting or framing a page element, changing the color of a photograph, grouping several elements together or positioning page elements so your attention is drawn in a certain direction. Let the following examples help you think about the plethora of ways you can create a strong focal point.

50 Things We Love about Christian

Create focal point with a close-up shot

One more thing we love...the way a close-up photo easily creates a strong focus for a page! Patricia's high-contrast, black-and-white photo enlargement magnifies her son's impish little grin and bright eyes, making it a challenge to look anywhere else first. The basic yet extensive journaling printed on white keeps the page balanced while not detracting from the photograph.

Patricia Anderson, Selah, Washington

Supplies: Patterned papers (Mustard Moon); tag (Making Memories); compass stamp (Stampabilities); rivets (Chatterbox); embossing powder; gray and tan cardstocks

50 THINGS We Love ABOUT CHRISTIAN:

1) How beautiful you are inside and out
2) Your big green eyes
3) Your incredible imagination
4) The way you dance
5) The way you sing
6) Your nose
7) The way you hop
8) Your expressive eyebrows
9) Your hearty, contagious laugh
10) Your sweet smile
11) Your handsome face
12) Your lean, strong body
13) Your love of reading
14) How smart you are
15) The way you talk to yourself
16) The way you say "I want to hode your hair"
17) The way you hold my hair
18) Your warm snuggles
19) Your politeness
20) The way you look like daddy
21) Your sweetness toward Ethy
22) Your protectiveness of your brother
23) Your love of me and daddy
24) Your love of school
25) Your empathy toward others
26) Your love of wrestling with daddy
27) The way you "talk" the parts of your toy figures
28) The way you make your toys argue with each other
29) Your love of play
30) Your sensitivity
31) Your kindness
32) Your compassionate nature
33) Your little curled toes (like daddy's)
34) Your long eyelashes
35) The way you have to talk to everyone
36) The way you say "I love you mommy"
37) How much you love your grandparents
38) How genuine you are
39) Your innocence

40) How sad you look when you cry
41) How you shrug your shoulders when you pout
42) How inquisitive you are
43) How you ask girls to marry you (at 3 years old)
44) How you talk about when you're a daddy someday
45) Your bravery toward making friends
46) Your understanding of difficult concepts
47) Your trap door memory
48) Your loyalty toward those you love
49) How precious you look while sleeping
50) That you're our son

California Coast

Let photo size dictate page focus

One large photo of the California waves makes a splash on this layout. By letting a large photo on the left take up the majority of the page, the eye can't help but dive in and then roll to the grouping of photos on the right-hand side. The silhouetted computer font title letters carefully carved into the top of the focal-point photo create a seamless look and draw even more attention to the enlargement.

Stacy Ford, Port Mugu, California

Supplies: Vellum; blue and white cardstocks; eyelets

Golf

Group photos to create focal point

If shown alone, any of the four golfing photos on Julie's layout would not be strong enough to create an impactful focal point. When cropped into identical squares and placed very close together in the center of a page, the four photos together create a successful focal point. Julie's arrangement is a good option when you have a group of photos in which none stands out the strongest of the batch.

Julie Mell, Tieri, Queensland, Australia

Supplies: Image-editing software

Shop Rules

Frame a photo to create focus

BEFORE: While this layout is nicely composed, the intended focal-point photo does not capture one's attention due to the bright yellow tape measure pulling the eye to the side of the page. While darker background paper attempts to frame the main photo, the photo itself is too similar of a shade to make the photo pop.

AFTER: The exact same photo, when accented with a bold wooden frame and metal corner braces, grounds the eye to create a successful focal point. The frame even gives the illusion that the photo has been enlarged.

Samantha Walker, Battle Ground, Washington

Supplies: Patterned vellum (Chatterbox); eyelets (Making Memories, Prym-Dritz); self-adhesive tape measure (Rockler); letter stamps (Stampin' Up!); wooden squares (Westrim); metal corner braces (from hardware store); cherry wood; acrylic varnish; blue, brown and red stamping inks; red, beige and shades of blue cardstocks; black pen

Because of You...

Allow line direction to highlight a photograph

Rays of dark green cardstock appear to "point" to a single color photograph, creating focal point through the direction of lines. In addition, to get the eye to travel in the right direction, Sharon used broken lines and eyelets. Starting from the top left-hand corner, following the lines and eyelets allows one to read the journaling in the correct order.

Sharon Whitehead, Vernon, British Colombia, Canada

Supplies: Pebble letters (K & Company); computer software (Printmaster by Broderbund); light and dark green cardstocks; eyelets

Where Will the World Take Us

Use optical illusion to emphasize a photo

Jodi arranged squares of monochromatic orange cardstock to give the illusion of a downward spiral, then mounted a single photo on top of the squares. The cardstock arrangement draws attention to the photo without having to enlarge it.

Jodi Amidei, Memory Makers Books

Supplies: Orange textured cardstocks (Bazzill); black patterned papers (Hot Off The Press); bottle caps and bottle cap stickers (Design Originals); letter stamps (Rubber Stampede); clear lacquer (Plaid); eyelets; twill tape; vellum

So Much to See out on the Lake
Contrast colors to create emphasis

To make one photo stand out from the rest, Shannon turned three photos black and white with image-editing software and left one in color. To further emphasize the color photo, she "silhouetted" the subject by erasing around the boy's head in a paint program, enabling the subject to stand out of the photo frame.

Shannon Freeman, Bellingham, Washington

Supplies: Image-editing software and paint program (Microsoft); drawing program (MicroGrafx Draw)

Your Shoes Are Dusty
Tint one section of a photo with color

When creating a page with only one photo, emphasize the most important parts of it by altering the color. To emphasize herself within a large group photo, Thena scanned her photo and used the tint function in image-editing software to color her dress and hair. She even chose a color for her dress that was similar to the actual dress color.

Thena Smith, Coronado, California

Supplies: Image-editing software (Microsoft Digital Image Pro)

Speeding Tickets

Layer photos to create emphasis

This focal-point photo bolts off this page due to the depth that is created by layering the same image in different sizes. Diana started by making an 8 x 10" black-and-white copy of a color photo. She then cropped the copy down to a 5 x 10" and used that as the background for the focal point. She matted a 4 x 6" color photo on black card-stock for emphasis, then layered it with a second cropped and matted copy of the same photo, which she attached with foam tape.

Diana Hudson, Bakersfield, California

Supplies: Patterned papers (Karen Foster Design); title letter stickers and label maker sticker (Pebbles); black ink; brad; staple; black cardstock; foam tape

PBJ

Let a title and journaling become your focal point

The size of the title letters and the patterned strips surrounding it make the title block stand out on this page. Tracy used large stamps to create the title, and the combination of patterns leads the eye to gobble it up. Journaling placed in a center column keep the focus on the story as well. The photo has been placed in the lower right corner of the page as a supporting element to the strong title and humorous story.

Tracy Miller, Fallston, Maryland

Supplies: Patterned papers (KI Memories); large letter stamps (www.earlychildhood.com); small letter stamps (Educational Insights); dark brown and tan cardstocks; brown stamping ink

Many scrapbookers have a natural tendency to fill in a blank area. After all, with the wide variety of stickers and premade embellishments out there, it's easy to keeping adding to a page until you simply can't fit anything else on it. But using space to display your photos and tell your story efficiently doesn't always mean filling up every inch on an 8½ x 11" or 12 x 12" page. Open space can be a very powerful tool to emphasize a favorite photo. It allows breathing room around the photo and thus draws your eye to it. Another way to utilize the space you have is to think beyond the borders of your background. Allowing elements to bleed off the edges of the page can create movement, energy and the illusion that there is more than what you see. Evaluate your photos, supplies and story beforehand to determine which concept of space will best communicate what you have to say.

A Boy and His Duck
Leave open space to create impact

Puppies need lots of room to play, as is demonstrated by the dynamics of this image surrounded by wide-open space. Heather formed a simple frame with patterned paper and brads to highlight the photo, and by choosing a light-toned background color, the photo becomes even more powerful. Offsetting the journaling to the right is one more effect that gives the pup his own "territory" and keeps the photo from competing for attention in the center of the page.

Heather Melzer, Yorkville, Illinois

Supplies: Yellow patterned papers (Mustard Moon); brads; black stamping ink

Joy

Focus on favorite photos by leaving space open

BEFORE: This page is drowning with many photos and elements that create a stressful energy. One's eye wants to chase after the subject rather than savor the emotion of joy that was intended.

BEFORE & AFTER

AFTER: Open space provides the calming effect and maximizes the intensity of the photos. The room to breathe on the page highlights the carefree spirit of a child at play and allows one to focus on the joy in her expression.

Elizabeth Ruuska, Rensselaer, Indiana

Supplies: Patterned cardstocks (Bazzill); rub-on word, woven corners (Making Memories); patterned papers (Scrapbook Wizard); label maker (Dymo); label holder (Magic Scraps); gingham ribbon (Close To My Heart); patterned vellum (K & Company); square punch (Family Treasures); leather strip (Rusty Pickle); woven "B" label (Me & My Big Ideas); brad

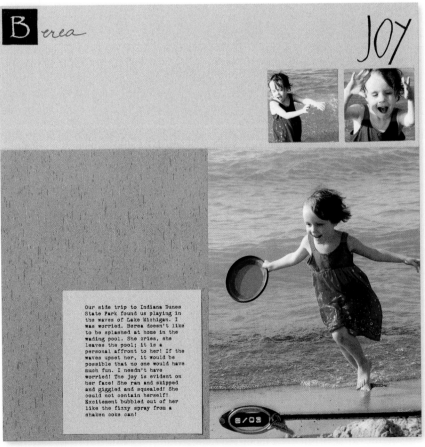

TIP: In design, extending images over the edges of your work surface is called bleeding. Bleeding tends to lead the eye off the page. Bleed elements over the edges of your scrapbook pages when you wish to create the illusion of a larger surface area.

brown-eyed girl

Madelyn has her daddy's eyes. They are big and brown, with thick dark lashes. She takes after her daddy in lots of ways. Her skin tone is perpetually tan. Her face shape has the same fullness in the cheeks. She has the same widow's peak hairline. She even has his long toes. She is like him in personality too. She is very concrete and practical. She likes things to be just so, and is quick to point out when things are not the way that they are supposed to be. I hope that she also has some of her daddy's best traits. His ability to work hard. His sense of humor. His loving nature and his loyalty. Not just his beautiful brown eyes.
Picture April 2003/Journaling June 2003

Brown-Eyed Girl

Create movement by extending circles off the page

This well-rounded page comes together as colored balls bounce off the edges of the page. When portions of a basic shape extend over the edges, one's mind completes the shape and creates the illusion of movement. Tracy gave more purpose to her circular design by shaping her journaling to fit inside one circle.

Tracy Miller, Fallston, Maryland

Supplies: Patterned paper (SEI); white, sage and tan cardstocks

The Story of Us

Create more space by exceeding page boundaries

Cherie wanted a title page for her family's album that seems to stretch beyond the focal-point photo. She created a collage in which certain elements slightly roll over the edges of the page, proving that you don't have to feel bound by the square space you have.

Cherie Ward, Colorado Springs, Colorado
Photo: Marilyn Eggleston, Colorado Springs, Colorado

Supplies: Patterned embossed paper (Paper Adventures); ephemera (www. LifetimeMoments.com); word tag (Chronicle Books); lock tag cut out and preprinted die cuts (EK Success); numbers sheet (source unknown); word epoxy sticker, faux wax seal and eyelets (Creative Imaginations); tag (Rusty Pickle); letter stickers (Stampendous); metal-rimmed tag; mesh; cork; black cardstock; magenta paper; fibers; buttons

Alaskan Spring Fishing

Simulate flow by exceeding page edges

Andrea let the river run through her layout...and then off to the ocean! Pieces of blue cardstock layered with foam tape and adorned with stickers emulate a river filled with salmon. By allowing the river to extend off both sides of the page, one gets the idea of continuous, moving water as well as the excitement of catching that big fish. The remainder of the page is kept simple to not overcrowd the layout. The hook and spring embellishments contribute to the idea of perpetual motion.

Andrea Lyn Vetten-Marley, Aurora, Colorado

Supplies: Texturizing paints (Krylon); stickers (Robin's Nest); wire; foam tape; hooks; brown, forest green, blue and beige cardstocks; embroidery floss

chapter 3

Creating Balance

At a young age, children learn to stack toy blocks in a balanced tower so they do not fall. Similarly, if a page contains all the elements of strong layout—clear, good-quality photographs, a strong title, innovative embellishments and interesting journaling—but isn't well-balanced, the page will usually fall flat. On a balanced scrapbook page, individual page elements are evenly distributed to complement one another. For example, the visual weight created by a large, vibrant photo placed in the upper left-hand corner of a page could be balanced by an embellishment, journaling block or other photo in the bottom right-hand corner.

Balance can be achieved in several different ways. In this chapter, learning about symmetrical and asymmetrical balance, unity, proper flow and rhythm will give you a plethora of options for designing balanced layouts.

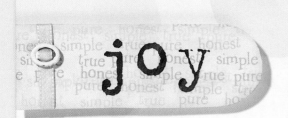

After a long day at work, I sometimes think of your bath time as a chore...hair to wash and a body to clean. I realize though, that this world would be a much happier place if we could all learn to find this much joy in what many consider a mundane task. Toria, you splash, soak and savor your time in the bubbles, and I pray that you will always continue to find joy in these everyday activities.

 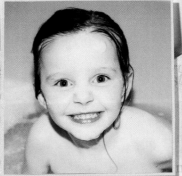 

Joy

Balance elements asymmetrically

This asymmetrical layout bubbles over with joyful emotion in an organized, well-balanced way. Denise used three small photo blocks to weigh down the bottom of the page, accented by a flower embellishment. The upper portion is balanced by the main large photo and the airy journaling bubble and title. The same flower accents bounce about the top to unify with the bottom and the bathtime-bubble paper.

Denise Tucker, Versailles, Indiana

Supplies: Bubble patterned paper (Bisous); text patterned paper (Creative Imaginations); metal label holder, rub-on letters and ribbon charms (Making Memories); ribbon (Offray); daisy punch (McGill); tacks (Chatterbox); chalk; acrylic paint; transparency; watch crystals; brads; foam core; foam tape; peach and white cardstocks

Design secret #8: Symmetry

Are you the type of person whose home is always orderly and scrapbook space is completely color-coordinated and organized? Or do you follow a more free-form, less structured philosophy of life? Your personality might reflect the type of scrapbook style you prefer. Symmetrical pages are ones in which one side of the page is the mirror image of the other. Each top and bottom corner has the metal embellishment. Two matted photos are placed vertically just left of the center, with the exact same photo treatment on the right side. Symmetrically balanced pages have an even number of page elements—usually two, four or six. Asymmetrical pages, on the other hand, while just as pleasing to the eye, are not mirror images of each other. They usually include an odd number of page elements. For example, a single photo, journaling block and decorative tag can be positioned in such a way that the elements balance each other, but they are not equal in number. Both are legitimate ways to arrange pages, and choosing one or the other can depend on the number of photos and accents you wish to use.

Like Father Like Son

Create symmetry on a single page

MaryJo included the same elements in the same arrangement on both sides of this page to create a symmetrical design. The design works well with two same-sized photos and also supports the concept of similarities between her husband and her son. She folded the four corners of her patterned background paper forward and secured each with a nailhead. At the top two corners, she hung decorated tags from the nailheads. A tape measure sticker divides the pages in two equal halves, making it a guide for equidistant photo, journaling and title placement. Concept inspired by Nancy Freebairn, Layton, Utah.

MaryJo Regier, Memory Makers Books

Supplies: Stickers (Frances Meyer, Karen Foster Design); red patterned paper (source unknown); saw die cuts (source unknown); blue, red and gold cardstocks; brads; string; nailheads

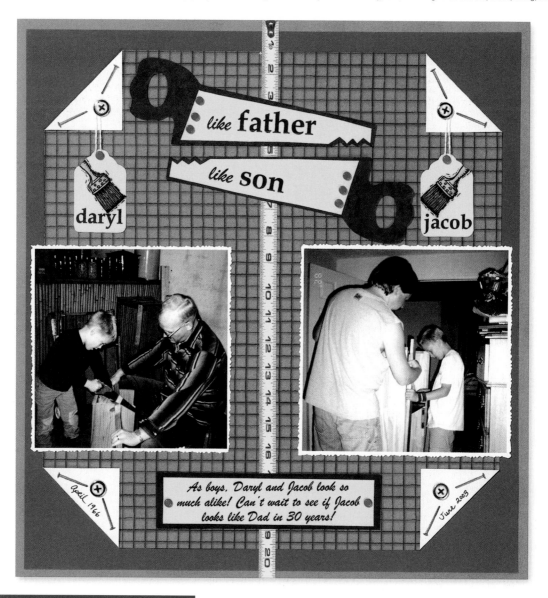

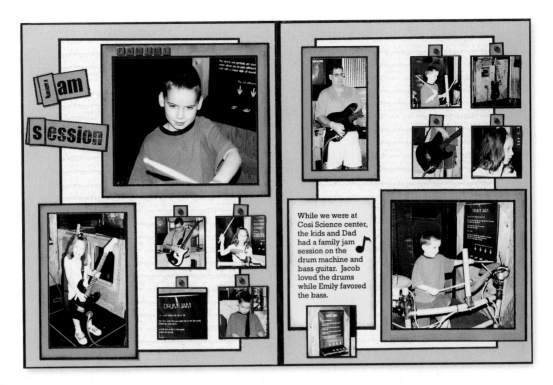

Jam Session

Design a spread with symmetrical elements

This family jam session makes perfect music to the eyes, utilizing a symmetrical layout comprised of four elements per page. On the left-hand page, the large photo and title at the top is repeated on the bottom right side, with a journaling block in place of the title. The vertical, orange-matted photo on the lower left-hand page can also be found at the top of the right-hand page, accompanied by four square photos with paper tabs each time.

Rhonda L. Pflugh, Canton, Ohio

Supplies: Patterned paper (source unknown); metal letter tiles (Making Memories); music note punch (EK Success); brads; black, mustard, olive and orange cardstocks; chalk

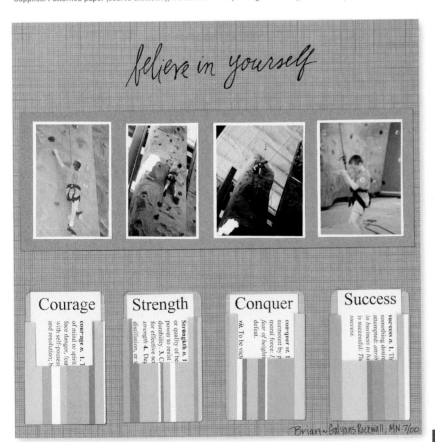

Believe in Yourself

Display journaling symmetrically

Laura included same-sized photos and pockets containing journaling on this page. Each pocket holds a card with definitions that reflect her son's character on one side and a personal note to her son on the other. She placed the photos and pockets in uniform columns across the page, creating a symmetrical layout.

Laura Henager, Bolingbrook, Illinois

Supplies: Brown plaid and striped paper (Chatterbox); pocket template (Deluxe Designs); rub-on letters (Making Memories); blue and white cardstocks; black pen

For You, Mommy

Consider arrangement of elements for asymmetry

BEFORE: When you have only three simple elements from which to build a pleasing asymmetrical layout—a photo, journaling block and flower embellishment—arrangement of these elements is very important. This layout appears extremely "heavy" on the left side, since all three elements are positioned there. One's eye tends to follow the baby's gaze and outstretched arm to the right side of the page, but there are no elements to anchor and balance the page once the eye reaches that side.

BEFORE & AFTER

AFTER: This page blossoms with eye-pleasing asymmetry, artfully arranged from left to right. Weight of page elements is well-distributed by placing the flower on the right-hand side and moving the title to the top right-hand corner. Enlarging the photo allows it to flow across the page instead of sitting stagnant in one spot.

Joanna Bolick, Fletcher, North Carolina

Supplies: Black, pastel green, pink and white textured cardstocks (Bazzill); metal-rimmed tag, brads and flowers (Making Memories)

Here you are again, another year later, chasing seagulls down the beach. I took a photo similiar to this of you last summer when you were learning to walk, chasing after the seagulls and I always loved that photo. So I was glad to find you chasing seagulls again this summer and quickly grabbed my camera! You would run for miles chasing them if mommy would let you! I look forward to many more summers of you chasing seagulls down the beach!

Chasing

Seagulls

live

Corey James
Summer 2003 - 2 years old

Chasing Seagulls
Arrange photos asymmetrically

Three different-sized photos were placed so they balance each other and save room for other page elements. Accompanying each photo is a piece of patterned paper and a bit of journaling, furthering the idea that asymmetry is achieved through an odd number of elements.

Tammy Gauck, Jenison, Michigan

Supplies: Blue patterned papers (Mustard Moon); Script patterned paper (7 Gypsies); photo corners and tag (Making Memories); epoxy word sticker (Creative Imaginations); fibers (Fibers By The Yard); shell charm (www.alltheextras.com); stamping ink; beads

Summer Fun

Place asymmetrical elements inside symmetrical ones

For a one-of-a-kind spread, Maureen combined both symmetrical and asymmetrical elements into one design. Asymmetry is present in the arrangement of the five inner page elements—two photos and three distinct sections of text. Surrounding these elements are symmetrical ones—a border of stripes and identical glass-marble adorned circles in the bottom left and top right sides of the spread. While distinctly different, all elements work together for a unified spread that makes a splash.

Maureen Spell, Carlsbad, New Mexico

Supplies: Rub-on title (Making Memories); letter stickers (Doodlebug Design); tiny glass marbles (Halcraft); vellum; light blue, aqua and medium blue cardstocks

One of the best things in summer is getting

WET

Nothing feels better than cool

water

Running down your back.
On this particular Indian summer day in September, you were told to water the flowers. When I looked outside, I saw how much fun you were having just spraying the water high in the air. You thought you were going to get in trouble, but I didn't mind you taking a moment to just have fun and play. It's ok to enjoy your job!

"He will be like rain falling on a mown field, like showers watering the earth" Psalm 79:6

SUMMER FUN

Bay Street Armoury

Combine symmetry and asymmetry

The foundation for Sharon's layout began with an enlarged photo of a building printed on white cardstock. The grand image traverses the two-page spread. Border strips embellished with brads across the top and bottom of the spread anchor the layout and create symmetry. She placed small photos strategically over parts of the background image she wanted to hide. These photos, along with three others places at different points, provide asymmetry on top of a symmetrical background.

Sharon Whitehead, Vernon, British Columbia, Canada

Supplies: Black, charcoal, maroon, white and gray cardstocks; brads; foam tape

Grace

Layer asymmetrical photos on a symmetrical background

A symmetrical backdrop of uniform, vertical stripes balances the asymmetrical arrangement of two baby photos and one journaling block. Photo mats offset from each picture contribute to the asymmetrical style.

Heather D. White, Riverton, Utah
Photos: Laura Ping, Fishers, Indiana

Supplies: Patterned papers (Rusty Pickle); fibers (Lion Brand); metal word washer, flower charm and eyelets (Making Memories); black chalk; white cardstock; pink and green papers; mesh drywall tape

[Grace]:
Pronounced 'grAs. Noun. 12th Century Middle English from Old French. 1. one of the most beautiful miracles in our lives; 2. one of the greatest joys we will ever know; 3. one of the reasons why there is a little extra sunshine, laughter and happiness in our world today.

Design secret #9: *Unity*

Whether you are designing single pages, two-page spreads or entire theme albums, the elements of your projects should look like they go together. This concept is called unity, and it's another tool to make your projects more cohesive and understandable. For graphic designers working on advertisements, if the headline, photo, copy and caption do not flow together well, the ad will seem confusing, it won't make a memorable impression on viewers and the message of the advertisement will be lost. There are lots of different way you can unify pages. For a single page, unify by repeating a certain embellishment or color in different areas. For a spread, let your title or a shape cross the gutter between the two pages. For a theme album, use the same or very similar layout for each page. Then, create a title and ending page that look similar as well.

Crimson Butterfly

Create unity by adding identical elements across a page

Karen punched small squares and graduated circles, then positioned them in different areas of her page to create unity. On opposite corners of the page, she adhered trios of squares near her photos. She arranged small, medium and large punched circles in curved shapes at the top and center of the page. Identical matting of photos and journaling provides even more harmony.

Karen Cobb, Victoria, British Columbia, Canada

Supplies: Patterned paper (Daisy D's); butterfly charm (Westrim); epoxy word sticker (Creative Imaginations); circle punches (Family Treasures); square punch (EK Success); circle die cut (Sizzix); mauve, tan and black papers; maroon ribbon; metal-rimmed tag; brad; skeleton leaf; foam tape

Fall Season

Unify a spread with patterned paper

By combining various blocks and strips of cardstocks, patterned papers and vellum in neutral tones, Mary unified this spread. The background papers are arranged the same on both pages, only one is turned on a 90-degree angle. Hand-drawn gold accents around photos, journaling and patterned papers further the consistent look of the spread.

Mary Walby, Royal Oak, Michigan

Supplies: Patterned papers and patterned vellum (EK Success); gold photo corners (Canson); gold paint pen (Marvy); beige, gray and white cardstocks; snaps

Being a Child

Allow a shape to bridge two pages

Cutting a large circle of journaling in two and adhering the pieces on either side of the page's gutter gave Michelle's spread a seamless, unified look. You naturally complete the circle shape in your mind, allowing your eye to flow easily over the page separation. Michele unified the look even more by repeating smaller circles across the spread.

Michelle Maret, South Bend, Indiana

Supplies: Blue patterned paper (Provo Craft); snowflake charms (Making Memories); letter die cuts (QuicKutz); gray-blue, white and black cardstocks; blue stamping ink; circle cutter; mesh; metal-rimmed tags; white and blue fibers

Family Album, Volume 10

Unify the design of beginning and ending album pages

One way to make an entire album seem unified, even if the content is very different, is by designing beginning and ending pages that have a similar stye. Michele began her family album by printing her title and a quote on yellow cardstock. She tore sections from patterned paper and placed it over the cardstock. To emphasize the idea of looking backward described in the quote, the page features the eyes of family members peeking out of black slide mounts. To make the ending page match the beginning, she used the same quote, more slide mounts and a similar torn-paper design. For variety, her patterned paper, though the same design, uses different colors, and the photos in the slide mounts focus on something each family member looked forward to in the coming year.

Michele Fischer, Longview, Washington

Supplies: Patterned papers (Colorbök); slide mounts; red, blue, green, orchid, lavender, light and medium blue cardstocks; black stamping ink; black pen

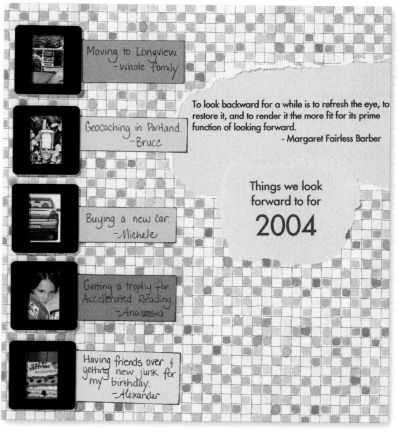

Table of Contents

Use the same fabric and accents for consistency in an album

When creating title and ending pages for her family album, Debra changed the overall layout, but kept a consistent feel with the use of fabric paper, decorated tags, coins, torn vellum journaling and the same font. She began the album by creating a table of contents of what's inside, then wrapped up the album with simple phrases and journaling that summarize happy memories while living in that home.

Debra Hendren, Royal Oak, Michigan

Supplies: Patterned fabric paper (K & Company); metal tags, eyelets, date and letter stamps (Making Memories); paper tags (7 Gypsies); fibers (Darice); cameo (Creative Block); pink and rust cardstocks; vellum; stamping ink; embossing ink; clear embossing powder; extra thick embossing powder; coins; watch parts; coin pendant holders

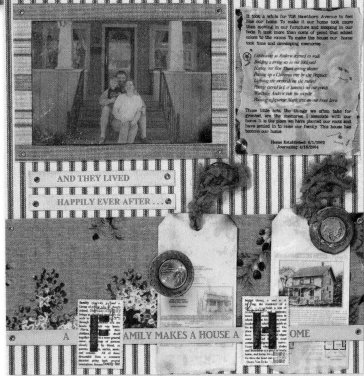

Christmas Album

Execute consistent page design for theme albums

Each small spread in Melissa's mini Christmas album has the same basic layout to unify the content. The left-hand pages are all made up of red and green patterned papers with a small strip of patterned paper at their intersection. Her journaling was printed on green while stamped images and paper holly leaves adorn the red section. Each right-hand page includes a 6 x 6" photo that Melissa enhanced by adding single words with image-editing software.

Melissa Smith, Northrichland, Texas

Supplies: Rudolph stamp series (Stampabilities); handmade green paper (Creative Papers Online); green patterned paper (Making Memories); red swirl paper (Printworks); red holly leaves paper (Paper Patch); image-editing software (Hewlett-Packard Creative Scrapbook Assistant); embossing ink; black stamping ink; extra thick embossing powder; green and white cardstocks; watercolor pencils

After visiting with Rudolph, we see The Big Guy! You're both usually a little shy, but glad to talk with Santa. This year, Sara, when Santa asked what you wanted for Christmas, you said, "Anything you would like is fine." Awww! Emily, your request is always the same: Anything Dalmatian!

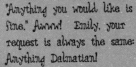

Wishes

Emily, when the Christmas season begins, the FIRST thing you want to do is see Rudolph at the mall. "Is Rudolph here yet, Mommy?" You love to watch his videos and sing "Rudolph the Red-Nosed Reindeer" around the house. As soon as he arrives at the mall, we go talk to him. Naturally, you always ask if you can sing him his song! I love those magical times with you.

Believe

Family Activities Album
Use similar colors, patterns and journaling style

To unify a family mini album, Jodi used shades of purple cardstock and patterned fabrics for the background of every page. In addition, she embossed the names of each activity on strips of vellum and printed each journaling block on white card-stock. She also inked the edges of each journaling block with purple ink and attached them with photo corners.

Jodi Amidei, Memory Makers Books

Supplies: Acrylic page accents (Creative Imaginations); dried flowers (Darice); album (7 Gypsies); chalk stamping ink (Clearsnap); purple and white cardstocks; fabrics; ribbon; photo corners; embossing powder

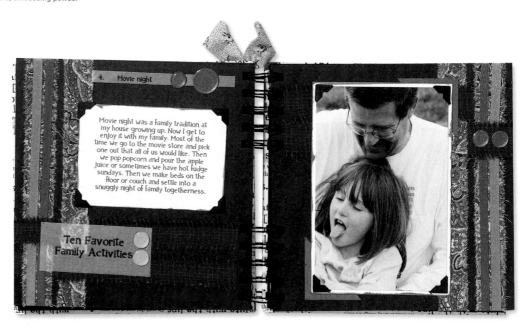

Ten Favorite Family Activities

One of the biggest joys of living in Colorado is a quick day trip to the mountains. Whether we are hiking, fishing, camping or just driving, day trips to the mountains are one of the best ways to spend a day. We have many favorite spots, like Rocky Mountain National Park, but most of the time it doesn't matter where we go. We just get in the car and head west. Where we end up is half the fun.

7. Trips to the mountains

9. Water fights

Ten Favorite Family Activities

During the hot summer months, you can always count on water fights at our house. It doesn't matter what starts it – it could be a short spray of the hose, and well placed water balloon, or a glass of ice water thrown over the shower curtain. It grows from there and before you know it, we are all drenched and laughing.

Ten Favorite Family Activities

Picnics in the park have been a family favorite since Haley was very small. Our most recent picnic was on a Sunday afternoon. We went to a large park not too far from where we live. We ate lunch, practiced Haley's batting, pitched horseshoes and played on the playground equipment. A fairly typical picnic in the park.

1. Picnics in the park

Magic in the Water

Watch placement of title words for improved readability

BEFORE: With the first word of this page title at the top right-hand corner and the rest in the middle, it is difficult to determine where the title begins. In addition, the page's subtitle, Dolphin Kisses, is separated by other words. Both of these placement choices disturb the flow of the page, leaving the reader unsure where to look first.

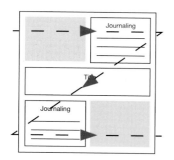

AFTER: Pamela placed the entire title through the center of the page. She combined both subtitle words and relocated the other journaling below them. Word placement is now more logical to how one's eye travels across a page. Thus, the page is easier to read and understand.

Pamela James, Ventura, California
Photos: Thom James, Ventura, California

Supplies: Blue swirl paper (Creative Imaginations); tag and letter stickers (EK Success); letter die cuts (Sizzix); wavy ruler (Creative Memories); blue, hot pink, light and dark aqua cardstocks; circle punch

TIP: When in doubt of how to arrange page elements so your design is easy to read, follow the z-flow method (shown above left). This is a method of page arrangement in which the eye enters the page from the left-hand side (such as when reading a book) and flows across the page in a "z" shape. Place the page element you want others to see or read first in the upper left-hand corner, then place other elements in a "z" shape down the page, based on importance.

A Dream Is a Wish

Arrange photos with subjects facing inward

BEFORE: The photos on this page were placed so that the subject's eyes are looking off the page in two different directions. Such placement leads the viewer's eyes off the page rather than focusing on its many details.

BEFORE & AFTER

AFTER: By simply switching the photos so the subject's gaze faces inward, the flow of the page is improved, and viewer's eye is drawn to the center of the page. In order to keep her layout balanced, Andrea swapped the placement of her journaling blocks and adjusted the positioning of her square brads.

Andrea Lyn Vetten-Marley, Aurora, Colorado

Supplies: Blue patterned papers (Tumblebeasts); music patterned papers (Design Originals); brown splatter paper (Pebbles); large square brads and dream charm (All My Memories); metal letters, small square brads and magnetic letter stamps (Making Memories); fluid chalk stamping ink (Clearsnap); embroidery floss; blue and brown thread; heart charm; black, blue, rust and brown cardstocks; chalk; brown and black stamping inks

The first thing that comes to mind when you think of rhythm is most likely music—not scrapbooking or design concepts. But when you repeat certain elements on a scrapbook page, visual rhythm is created. Repeating page elements such as photos, embellishments, shape or techniques create familiarity and often the illusion of movement. This will make your layouts more visually interesting. In fact, when in doubt about how to make a page look balanced, repeating an element is almost always a safe bet. Variation is another key component to creating rhythm. Repeating an element is a good start, but to keep the layout exciting, it's good to include variety within the repeated elements. The following examples show how this can be achieved in many different ways.

Learning to Play the Piano

Repeat photos to create rhythm

Leah cropped three similar photos to the same size and stacked them vertically alongside her focal-point photo. Her son's different poses and facial expressions provide variation within a repeating photo pattern. Her use of neutral papers helps her son's bright red shirt pop off the page, reinforcing the repetition.

Leah Fung, San Diego, California

Supplies: Striped paper and round tag (Chatterbox); black and tan cardstocks; black photo corners; snap; clock hand

Jump

Display action photos in a sequence

Using her digital camera, Tammy photographed her daughter jumping over a spray of water. She highlighted Danielle's intense action and agility by repeating sequential photos across the page. She cropped the photos to the same size and framed them in black cardstock to resemble a film strip.

Tammy Gauck, Jenison, Michigan

Supplies: Orange flower paper (Karen Foster Design); black, evergreen, white and orange cardstocks; vellum; buttons

Remember

Echo a single element across the page

Sam designed this layout using just one photo printed in several different sizes. To begin, she enlarged the original, printed it on a clear transparency and then adhered it to the page under a preprinted transparency. Simple embellishments such as a clear slide mount, photo corners and matting accent several of the photos. Repeating the photo while varying the size achieves a serene feel while contributing to the overall flow and cadence of the page.

Sam Cousins, Trumbull, Connecticut

Supplies: Patterned transparency (Creative Imaginations); letter stickers (Colorbök, EK Success, Sticker Studio); letter and number stamps (Making Memories); clear slide mount, photo corners and tile stickers (EK Success); red, white and black cardstocks; black stamping ink; fibers; heart charm

Family Is a Treasure
Repeat embellishments across a spread

Punched flowers combined with buttons frolic across Heather's spread to show rhythm through the repetition of embellishments. Before adhering the flowers, she tore blocks of patterned papers and yellow vellum and placed them over blue cardstock. Long strips of blue vellum serve as backdrops for titles and coordinate with her flower embellishments.

Heather Polacek, Niles, Ohio

Supplies: Flower patterned paper (KI Memories); flower and circle punches (EK Success); letter stickers (Creative Imaginations); metal-rimmed tags (Making Memories); yellow, dark blue and pastel blue vellums; dark blue and cream cardstocks; buttons; brads

My Wishes for You
Repeat stamped images

Terri stamped Chinese symbols onto cardstock and displayed them down the right side of the page. Red and black mats frame each image identically. The slightly curled edges of the black matting give it definition against the black background.

Terri Daugherty, Chesterfield, Virginia

Supplies: Chinese stamps (Hero Arts); fan button (Blumenthal Lansing); red, white and black cardstocks; black stamping ink; white thread; date stamp

Talk, Talk

Echo shapes in different sizes

Tracy created rhythm on this page by repeating circles in various sizes. Each circle serves a slightly different purpose on the page: One serves as a backdrop for the page title, another houses journaling, while smaller circles were used for corner accents. The overlap of the circles contributes to the design's smooth rhythm.

Tracy Miller, Fallston, Maryland

Supplies: Vellum letter stickers (Mrs. Grossman's); flower tag (KI Memories); circle template (Provo Craft); black, white and pale yellow cardstocks

Beautiful

Include multiple decorated tags

The rhythm of this page occurs through the repetition of tags across the dark background. Christine made each tag unique by embellishing them somewhat differently. Along with photos, she incorporated mesh, cork, letter stamps, mica and more for variation amongst the repetition.

Christine Brown, Hanover, Minnesota

Supplies: Mesh and cork papers (Magenta); letter stamps (PSX Design); beads (EK Success); alphabet tile letters (Limited Edition Rubber Stamps); vellum tags, paper yarn and metal letters (Making Memories); buttons (Hillcreek Designs); mesh (Magic Mesh); skeleton leaves (Graphic Products Corp.); black, teal, red, green and yellow papers; foam core; screws; pressed flowers; mica; black stamping ink; nailheads; black and white pens; wire; screen mesh; photo corners; eyelets; tassel; fibers; chalk

Chapter 4

Adding Finesse

Once you've learned the rules and design concepts associated with color, layout and balance, it's time to push the limits of creativity by adding that little something extra. The expressions "it's the little things that count" and "God is in the details" could be used to describe what finishing touches do to your pages. From tiny stitches in the corners to a distressed background design, the details you add can make your memories even more special.

On the following pages, you'll be inspired to add finesse with lettering, visual and tactile texture and conceptual embellishments. Combining these ideas with the concepts you've already learned will make you an even stronger page designer.

A Walk in the Fall

Strengthen a page with carefully chosen embellishments

To dress up her fall page design, Michelle used simple velvet leaves to support the content her photos. She colored each leaf with copper metallic rub-ons and gold acrylic paint, emulating her leaf patterned paper. The addition of burlap and crumpled paper adds to the natural feel of the page.

Michelle Pesce, Arvada, Colorado

Supplies: Leaf patterned paper (Scrap-Ease); leather patterned paper (Club Scrap); transparency (Grafix); velvet leaves (Stampington & Company); metallic rub-ons (Craf-T); gold acrylic paint (Plaid); evergreen and rust cardstocks; chalk; burlap; foam tape

Designers put as much thought into choosing the right fonts for a project as they do into the colors and images. Because it's the stories behind your scrapbook pages that future generations will want to know about most, fonts and lettering are all the more crucial in scrapbook design. It's important to choose lettering styles that suit the content, such as a elegant script style for a wedding page. And while the number of downloadable computer fonts on the Internet make experimenting with lettering even more exciting, remember to reign yourself in. Too many fonts can make a page difficult to read. Moreover, basic journaling blocks are best when displayed in standard, less decorative fonts for the same reason. Have fun with fonts and lettering, but know when to say "when."

Tiki Hut

Add textured letters to support a theme

Darlene cut and glued cane reeds over paper letters to make a title that relates to the Tiki hut in which her husband and daughter were photographed. She further embellished the title letters by stitching short pieces of raffia between two sheets of cardstock on her sewing machine to create the look of the Tiki roof. Smaller bits of journaling, written on stamped paper and cut to look like primitive signs, reflect her theme.

Darlene Johnson Calloway, Tequesta, Florida

Supplies: Shadow letter die cuts (Sizzix); wooden crate stamp (Stampington & Company); light, medium and dark brown cardstocks; sepia stamping ink; raffia; tall cane reeds; hemp cord; foam tape; brown pen

Toledo

Design a title to suit photo content

BEFORE: This understated title gets lost next to the elaborate travel photos. While clear and easy to read, the title does not communicate anything about the page's content.

AFTER: Samantha's new title, full of travel-themed embellishments, supports the theme and makes the page exciting. To form the letter T, she silhouette cut a sword from a photograph and mounted it on a red paper background. She combined a letter stamp used in the background with scanned travel images and a Spanish coin to dress up the rest of the title.

Samantha Walker, Battle Ground, Washington

Supplies: Travel stamp set, letter stamps and tags (Stampin' Up!); photo paper (Hewlett-Packard); image-editing software; red, white and cream cardstocks; brown and black stamping ink; Spanish coin; scanned images of coins, postage stamps and envelopes

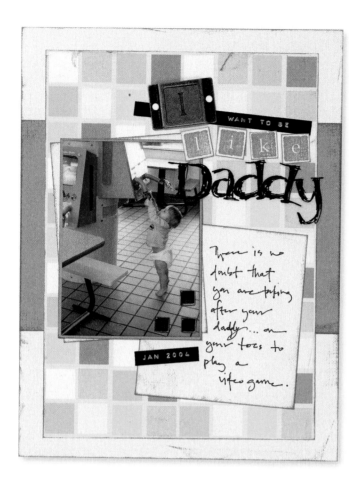

I Want to Be Like Daddy
Mix lettering types of different media

Rosemary combined several letter styles in different media for this page. Her title is made up of a metal letter, a label maker strip, stamping and sticker letters to create interest. The mixture of styles supports the playful look of the page.

Rosemary Waits, Mustang, Oklahoma

Supplies: Block patterned paper (Chatterbox); metal letter charm and label holder (Making Memories); letter stamps (Hero Arts); letter stickers (Wordsworth); label maker (Dymo); brown stamping ink; brads; cream and rust cardstocks

Firestorm
Use fonts and color to enhance emotion

A bold, dramatic title, combined with Sharon's powerful photos, solidify the mood of this spread. The font she chose might call to mind the ashes left behind after a raging blaze is extinguished. Choosing red—a warm, aggressive color—and printing title words in a large point size reinforce the turmoil seen on the page.

Sharon Whitehead, Vernon, British Columbia, Canada

Supplies: Square nailheads (www.scrapnpaper.com); black and red cardstocks

Lil' Chatterbox
Emphasize words with size

By enlarging one word of her title and stamping another with small letters, Jennifer gave the word "chatterbox" weight and significance, which set the scene for her page theme. To emphasize Connor's first words without competing with the title, she printed them on light cardstock rather than dark, cut them into individual strips and accented each with a button to set it apart. The font she chose is easy to read, and letters that stray from the baseline communicate a youthful feel.

Jennifer Bourgeault, Macomb Township, Michigan
Photo: My Photographer, Sterling Heights, Michigan

Supplies: Plaid papers (Chatterbox); letter stamps (PSX Design); buttons (Hero Arts); brown and white cardstocks; black stamping ink; chalk

TIP: If you like to incorporate your own handwriting on scrapbook pages but have trouble with consistent spacing and straight lines, type your journaling first. When you've arranged the typed journaling exactly as you want it, lay a sheet of vellum over the type and trace over each letter.

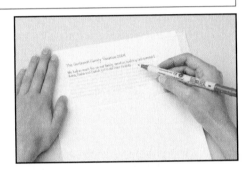

Caught Red-Handed
Use lettering to create a focal point

Michelle proves that lettering can become the focal point of the page and not just a supporting element. The black cut-out letters placed on a large red circle over a simple background immediately demand one's attention. In addition, the title's design reinforces the red color throughout the spread as well as the humorous subject matter.

Michelle Ballard, Hagerstown, Maryland

Supplies: Circle paper clip (Target); red, black, taupe and cream cardstocks; black pen

Choosing Fonts

Only a century ago, typesetters stayed busy attaching metal letter ends to tiny wooden blocks in order to print on newspaper. As technology advanced, so did typesetting and the world of graphic arts. Today, companies pay big bucks to have the "right" fonts complementing their products. As scrapbookers, you don't have to pay big bucks to accent your pages—just search the Internet. Start by typing "fonts" into a search engine and see what comes up. After finding what you want, it's important to choose fonts that fit your page theme. Just as you probably wouldn't hang floral curtains in your husband's office, a romantic script font would not be the best choice for a "Mud Buddies" page. The categories and samples below will help you choose fonts that are theme- and style-appropriate.

Playful

Scrubadoo
www.1001freefonts.com

BUBBLE GUM ROCK
www.dafont.com

baby kruffy
www.dafont.com

to be continued
www.dafont.com

Baveuse
www.1001freefonts.com

ULTIMATUM
www.1001freefonts.com

Retro

SWINKYDAD
www.dafont.com

HAMBURGER MENU
www.fontdiner.com

Mister Television
www.fontdiner.com

Starburst Lanes
www.fontdiner.com

International Palms
www.fontdiner.com

CORNFED
www.dafont.com

Stamped/Handmade Looks

Rubber stamp
www.fontface.com

copystruct bold
www.dafont.com

MALERMEISTER
www.dafont.com

RUBBERMAID
www.dafont.com

DYMOFONTINVERS
www.dafont.com

JJ STENCIL
www.dafont.com

Whimsical

Angelica
www.dafont.com

Clastic Wrath
www.fontface.com

floozy
www.dafont.com

curly coryphaeus
www.dafont.com

Eskargot
www.dafont.com

Elegant

Lauren Script
www.dafont.com

Fontleroy Brown
www.dafont.com

FreeBooter
www.fontconnection.com

BlackJack
www.fontface.com

Using Fonts

After finding the fonts that are a great fit, keep these guidelines in mind to communicate your messages clearly.

• The point size of your title should be larger than your journaling. Consider 14-point type for journaling, but think big for an impactful title.

• Use the bold and italic options to place emphasis on certain words and help break up large amounts of running text.

• Consider using serif fonts (those that have fine lines finishing off the main strokes of letters) for heavily journaled pages. Generally, they are considered easier on the eyes because they flow together smoothly.

• Unique fonts with decorative details, known as display fonts, are best for titles. Display fonts can be hard to read if printed too small or when used for a large block of text.

• In general, limit the number of fonts you use on a page to about three. Too many can be confusing and difficult to read.

Chicago

Add letter-shaped photos to establish a focal point

To incorporate the many skyline photos Dawn took in Chicago, she used a template to cut them into letter shapes. Mounting each letter on blue cardstock and adhering them with foam tape visually separates the title from other page elements, thus creating focal point.

Dawn Harp, Kansas City, Missouri

Supplies: Letter template (C-Thru Ruler); sky blue, navy blue and white cardstocks; square punch; brads; vellum; chalk; foam tape; scanned image of map; memorabilia

TIP: If your photographs are slightly dark or blurry and you'd rather not enlarge one for a photographic focal point, design your title with bright colors or a bold font so that it can serve as the focus of your page.

You Are So Incredible Matthew

Incorporate title words in a journaling block

To create her title, Jlyne modified five words within her journaling block. She changed the font from a small script style to larger, bold text. This technique also adds interest to the page by breaking up the large block of text.

Jlyne Hanback, Biloxi, Mississippi

Supplies: Weathered cream paper (Paper Loft); brown patterned paper and black nailheads (Chatterbox); photo holders (7 Gypsies); ribbon and metal label holder (Making Memories); tan cardstock; black pen

Design secret #12: *Texture*

These days, it seems scrapbookers know no boundaries when it comes to texture. Everything is lumpy and bumpy, proving that scrapbook pages can appeal to our fingertips as much as they do to our eyes. Could it be that as creative people, scrapbookers feel limited by the flat surface of the page, and build the page upward to give themselves more creative space? If you like the look of texture but don't care for the bulk, consider adding visual texture to your pages. This can be done by using certain patterned papers. Adding "shadows" to your pages can also create the illusion of depth. While the possibilities are endless for tactile texture, if it's the look of texture you want, lumpy pages aren't your only option.

Spring

Add patterned papers for a textured look

Vicki used different patterned papers to create a visually textured background without bulk. One pattern has the look of cracked paint and another, the look of floral fabric. To add more depth and coordinate with the patterns, Vicki crumpled and flattened solid magenta paper and inked the edges of pale pink paper.

Vicki Harvey, Champlin, Minnesota

Supplies: Floral patterned paper (K & Company); crackle patterned paper (Carolee's Creations); magenta, pale pink, mauve and evergreen cardstocks; mulberry paper; mauve stamping ink; white thread; craft knife; silver pen

brightly colored tulips and daffodils

smelling the fresh air

walking around Lake Harriet

spending time outside without a coat

warm, sunny days after a long Minnesota winter

Erin - May 2002

The Cutest Fans

Include a variety of patterns for visual texture

BEFORE: Solid cardstocks form the foundation of this page, paired with simple shapes, a large focal-point photo and themed stickers.

AFTER: When multiple patterns replace solid cardstocks, a rugged, textured look is added to the design—an appropriate choice for both baseball and masculine themes. The page has much more pizazz and the elements seem to cry out, "play ball!"

Jennifer Bourgeault, Macomb Township, Michigan

Supplies: Baseball stickers (S.R.M. Press); baseball patterned paper and letter stickers (Sticker Studio); red crackle paper and striped paper (Me & My Big Ideas); leather patterned paper (Karen Foster Design); newsprint patterned paper (Sweetwater); corrugated cardboard patterned paper (Pebbles); copper letters and metal-rimmed tags (Making Memories); dark brown, medium brown, black, white, red and gray cardstocks

Butterfly

Add shadows to create the illusion of depth

With image-editing software, Sheila achieved many textured looks on this page. For her page background, she applied colored pencil and embossing filters to dark pink, then inserted an enlarged photo and applied a watercolor filter. To smaller photos placed over the background, Sheila added shadows for more depth.

Sheila McIntosh Dixon, Milton, Florida

Supplies: Image-editing software (Microsoft Digital Image Pro)

Visual vs. Tactile Texture

Whether you love lumpy-bumpy pages or want a textured look without the bulk, here are some ways to achieve both.

Creating Visual Texture

- patterned paper/preprinted product
- overlapping/layering papers
- optical illusion (the look of 3-D blocks, stair steps, etc. formed with paper)
- matting
- shading with chalk/ink
- digital shadow effects

Creating Tactile Texture

- dry and wet embossing
- crumpling paper/distressing
- fabric
- mesh
- metal embellishments
- fibers/ribbon
- foam tape
- fold-out and pull-out elements
- buttons/pebbles

Autumn

Include a fold-out element for texture

The hinges attached to this focal-point photo lift to reveal another image of Anna's son as well as a block of journaling. Not only does this element add texture, it adds flexibility to the design. Anna's page title also incorporates many different textured elements such as metal, fabric and plastic.

Anna Burgess, Clarksville, Tennessee

Supplies: Rust patterned paper (Karen Foster Design); metal sheet (K & S Metals); engraving tool and antique hinges (Magic Scraps); metal-rimmed tags, metal corner accents, metal letter and letter pebble (Making Memories); adhesive hanging tags (Bulldog Hardware); metal mesh (Scrapyard 329); circle letter rub-ons (Creative Imaginations); letter stickers (Colorbök); letter stamps (PSX Design); orange fibers; olive and rust cardstocks; black stamping ink; eyelets; safety pin; brads; burlap; corduroy fabric; metallic rub-ons; chalk

The Three "P's" of Summer

Create depth with foam core

Using a craft knife, Tracey cut out three windows from blue cardstock to fit her photos. She then cut strips of foam core and adhered them to the back of the blue. Then she adhered her photos to white cardstock and layered the blue cardstock with foam core over it. To create a wet look and include additional texture, Tracey applied embossing ink and powder to the blue cardstock and heated it.

Tracey Pagano, North Caldwell, New Jersey

Supplies: Blue and white textured cardstocks (Bazzill); stitched tin squares and magnetic date stamp (Making Memories); letter stamps (PSX Design); embossing ink; pigment powder; embossing powder; square punch; vellum; buttons; brads; twine; embroidery floss; craft knife

Thoughtful

Mimic nature's texture with punches

Emulating the vines from her photo, Shannon cut sections of paper yarn for the stems and hand-sewed them to the page with nylon thread. From evergreen cardstock, she punched individual leaves, folded each leaf, embellished it with chalk and pen and adhered it to the page with foam tape.

Shannon Taylor, Bristol, Tennessee
Photo: Chris Smith, Roanoke, Virginia

Supplies: Wood veneer sheet (source unknown); green paper yarn (Making Memories); leaf punch (Emagination Crafts); nylon thread; black, evergreen and tan cardstocks; black pen; chalk; foam tape

Indian Summer
Crumple paper for texture

Crumpled paper often means you need to make a trip to the trash can, but for page design, it's a way to add subtle texture to your pages. Michelle used this technique on her photo mats and journaling blocks. To help them lie as flat as possible, she sewed some of the pieces together. To create the appearance of more texture, she randomly blotted the papers with watermark ink. This technique deepened the color of the papers, creating the look of shadows.

Michelle Pendleton, Colorado Springs, Colorado

Supplies: Paper tiles and rub-on letters (Creative Imaginations); watermark stamping ink (Tsukineko); date and letter stamps and ribbon (Making Memories); chalk stamping ink (Clearsnap); evergreen, avocado, gold and brown cardstocks; eyelet; embroidery floss

When I Grow Up...
Add an accordion album to a page

Andrea's mini accordion album adds texture to her page, as well as detail and information. To create the book, she folded a cardstock strip into four equal sections. This gave her eight panels to decorate with journaling, photos, letter stickers, stamps, trinkets and more. The book hangs on the page by a crocheted cord laced through eyelets. The addition of antique buttons and Andrea's crocheted doilies brings more rich textures to the page.

Andrea Lyn Vetten-Marley, Aurora, Colorado

Supplies: Olive wood-grain patterned paper (Pebbles); measuring tape paper, antique book papers, kids paper and old reader patterned papers (Design Originals); spelling book and tan alphabet patterned papers (7 Gypsies); letter stamps (EK Success); chalk stamping ink (Clearsnap); white pencil; brown stamping ink; vintage crochet thread; crochet needle; buttons, eyelets; black, white and evergreen cardstocks; faux playing cards; dark brown and ivory thread

Embellishing your pages with metals, beads, buttons, fibers and more is half the fun—sometimes the most fun—of scrapbooking. Embellishment plays an important role in scrapbook design, but keeping design concepts in mind, it is important that your embellishments have purpose. If there is a reason, or concept, behind every embellishment you use, you might discover the number of items you are adding is less, but the impact of the page is stronger. For example, fibers are lots of fun, but fibers on a page of a cat playing with a ball of yarn is more than fun—it's a concept that matches the content of your page. The following examples show how readers use all types of embellishments to support their page themes.

Blue Jean Baby

Complement a theme with a fabric pocket

Heather's blue jean pocket embellishment serves a dual purpose—it supports the theme of her photos and makes a great place for pull-out journaling. She cut the pocket from a pair of secondhand jeans purchased for $1. After removing the pocket, she adhered it to the page and used it as a backdrop for two more photos.

Heather Preckel, Swannanoa, North Carolina

Supplies: Blue patterned paper (Books by Hand); Scrabble letters (Hasbro Corporation); beads (On The Surface); walnut ink (Postmodern Designs); tan, blue and white cardstocks; brads; eyelets; wire; jean pocket

Sweet

Coordinate vintage embellishments

Inspired by the photo, Janel sought out embellishments at her local scrapbooking store to create this layout. When she found old-fashioned candy labels, they reminded her of her great-niece's sucker. She coordinated the labels with vintage newspaper-clipping patterned paper, linen paper and touches of red and gingham ribbon. Her embellishments go well together, and support her sugary sweet theme.

Janel Brown, Longmont, Colorado

Supplies: Newspaper clipping patterned paper, linen patterned paper and word concho (7 Gypsies); vintage label stickers (Heart & Home); letter die cuts (Sizzix); black cardstock; gingham ribbon; brads; black and red corrugated cardstocks

Let's Jamba

Mimic product design with vellum and lacquer

Based on the images from a Jamba Juice cup, Dana drew fruit shapes with a black pen, then traced over her pen lines with clear lacquer. She says she likes to use this type of adhesive for quick and easy "embossed" looks. Along with vibrant vellums, she chose citrus-colored background papers and attached her fruit accents to the page with brightly colored eyelets.

Dana Matsukawa, Kailua, Hawaii

Supplies: Green speckled and orange swirl papers (Provo Craft); letter stickers (Creative Imaginations); tag stickers (Doodlebug Design); orange, green, red, yellow and purple vellums (Autumn Leaves); clear lacquer (JudiKins); metal-rimmed tags; square punch; eyelets; black pen; foam tape

The Measure of a Man

Back a title with appropriate premade product

Mecque used a ruler sticker under her transparency title to enhance the idea of measuring her husband's worth. In addition, natural elements such as mica, coastal netting and earth-toned patterned paper convey a masculine, outdoorsy feel to coordinate with her outdoor photos.

Mecque Leonard, Jordan, Minnesota

Supplies: Brown patterned paper (Carolee's Creations); mica and coastal netting (www.alteredpages.com); ruler sticker (EK Success); letter stamps (Hero Arts); rub-on letters (Creative Imaginations); black, brown and white cardstocks; black stamping ink; brads; transparency; foam tape; spray adhesive

Foam Fight

Embellish older photos with childhood crafts

As Linda scrapbooked photos of her younger days at camp, she remembered making lanyards and working with plastic lacing during arts and crafts time. She used elements from those crafts as page embellishments. Then, using a palette knife, Linda scooped small piles of art foam and placed them around the page to mimic the shaving cream in her photos. Her title letters were cut from a foam sheet to stick with the camp crafts theme.

Linda Mallon, Tucson, Arizona

Supplies: Art foam (DecoArt); foam sheet (Fibre Craft); lettering template (Scrap Pagerz); plastic laces (Pepperell); plastic canvas (Darice); lanyard hook (Cousin); patterned vellum (source unknown); sea foam green, white and turquoise cardstocks; eyelet; pony beads; sock hangers; chalk

Brianna Lyn

Emphasize femininity with fabric and lace

Andrea collected various supplies from her sewing box for this page. Eyelet lace, satin ribbon and rickrack run across the page to provide a framing effect, and coordinate well with the lacy dress in the photographs. Patterned papers that have been moistened, crumbled and ironed are sewn to the background.

Andrea Lyn Vetten-Marley, Aurora, Colorado

Supplies: Striped paper (Chatterbox); floral paper (source unknown); letter stamps (All Night Media); thank you stamp (PSX Design); twill tape definition (7 Gypsies); covered buttons; fabric; rickrack; satin roses; blue satin ribbon; buttons; safety pins; black pen; thread; ribbon flowers; lace flowers

3-D Storage and Handling

Sometimes the conceptual embellishments that best suit your theme are 3-D items, which will add weight and bulk to your albums, and can damage pages if you are not careful. Consider the following points before adding 3-D embellishments to your pages.

• Always store albums upright on a bookshelf so the pressure of 3-D items does not damage other pages.

• Use extra-sturdy cardstock for your background or mount the page on foam core to keep it from bending.

• When possible, plan your albums around 3-D items. Do not place photos directly across from embellishments on a facing page.

• Always limit the number of heavy items and pair them with light supplies such as ribbons or fibers.

• For post-bound albums or three-ring binders, consider adding thin strips of cardboard in the binding to space pages apart. You won't be able to fit as many pages in your album, but 3-D items will have more room to breathe.

• Purchase page protectors made specifically for 3-D items. For example, Protect-A-Page protectors by Dolphin Enterprises (shown) are ¼" deep with a front flap that closes like a book, allowing plenty of room for 3-D items inside.

First Frost

Create a frosted look with clear glass marbles

Heidi replicated the image of frost settling in the veins of leaves that she so often sees in the fall. Using silk leaves in fall colors, she glued rows of tiny glass marbles to each with strong liquid adhesive. To complete her title, she layered die-cut letters over the leaves and applied more marbles to each letter.

Heidi Summers, Missoula, Montana

Supplies: Plaid paper (Bo-Bunny Press); letter die cuts (Sizzix); silk leaves (Wal-Mart); vellum; burgundy, green, rust and pumpkin cardstocks; brads; embossing powder; tiny glass marbles

Winds

Accentuate outdoor photos with natural adornments

Anne's family photos taken in a wheat field shine forth when surrounded by natural elements such as fibers, wheat, burlap and raffia. Layered earth-toned papers used for photo mats, journaling and title blocks bring more of an organic look to the page.

Anne Pearson, Heber, Utah

Supplies: Parchment patterned paper (Karen Foster Design); evergreen and gold patterned papers (All My Memories); red linen patterned paper (K & Company); leaf and embrace charms (Blue Moon Beads); fibers; white speckled cardstock; burlap; raffia; brass eyelets; chalk; wheat stalk

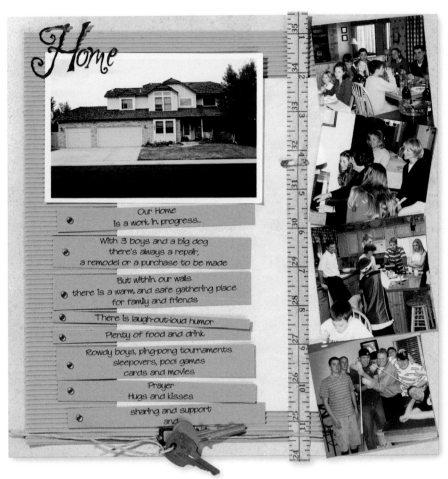

Home

Enhance household layouts with found items

By collecting simple household objects and combining them with other scrapbooking elements, Janell's page reflects the atmosphere around her house. A set of keys, a safety pin, corrugated cardstock and a ruler sticker communicate the point from Janell's journaling that a home is always a work in progress.

Janell Knudson, Littleton, Colorado

Supplies: Speckled green paper (Sweetwater); peach script paper (Amscan); ruler sticker (EK Success); letter stickers (Creative Imaginations); brown cardstock; corrugated cardstock; brads; keys; safety pin; paper label holder; twine

TIP: Sometimes the conceptual embellishment that best suits a page will not be found in your scrapbook supplies. Depending on your page topic, search the rooms of your home for a found object that fits, such as old jewelry, keys, product packing, etc.

Remember, Reflect

Use mirrors for a page of somber reflection

Diana thought that mirrors were the perfect embellishment for a page about remembering and reflecting on the Oklahoma City bombing tragedy. She created her title by stamping and embossing on small mirrored tiles. The content of the photos emphasizes the reflection theme even more, and the use of mirrors supports this idea.

Diana Hudson, Bakersfield, California

Supplies: Square mirrors (JewelCraft); letter stamps (Hero Arts); square nailheads (Hirschberg Schutz & Co.); black and cream cardstocks; metal label holder; vellum; brads; black stamping ink; clear embossing powder

Chapter

5

Applying All Concepts

As you create pages keeping color, layout, balance and finesse in mind, you'll soon discover that these concepts rarely work independently of one another. Often, several different concepts can be identified on one page. As you practice and apply them, they will start to become instinctive as you create. In this gallery, many of the design concepts discussed throughout this book are identified. Browse through them, and try to pinpoint other concepts that might not be mentioned.

Christmas Sunset

Create mood through color

Sam's use of warm analogous colors, pink and orange, creates a mood of excitement and energy appropriate for the night before Christmas, even though they are nontraditional for the season. Paired with photos of a stunning sunset, Sam's colors also lend a serene feel.

Sam Cousins, Trumbull, Connecticut

Supplies: Patterned papers, rub-on letters, metal 2003 tag, star eyelet, photo anchors and brads (Making Memories); letter stickers (Chatterbox, Creative Imaginations, Sticker Studio); black stamping ink; fibers

Time

Group multiple photos to create a single focal point

Using image-editing software, Martha cropped six photos of her son to an equal size. She combined them on a 3 x 2" grid, then printed them as one unit. When grouped, the six small photos serve as the focal point of the page. She triple matted the image to give it even more weight. Square preprinted accents placed along the bottom of the page balance the design.

Martha Crowther, Salem, New Hampshire

Supplies: Clock face paper and clock die cuts (KI Memories); fibers (Fibers By The Yard); image-editing software (Hewlett-Packard Photo Printing); spring green, black and white cardstocks

World Trade Center

Build a layout on a three-column grid

Dividing her first page into vertical thirds, Pam placed a vertical panoramic photo in the center column. Around that she arranged three smaller snapshots, a journaling block and the title. For the right-hand page, she broke the three-column structure into smaller segments. Using the stripes on her background paper as a guide, she cropped photos into thin strips and placed them between the stripes. The repeated pattern creates visual rhythm, with the center photo serving as variation within that rhythm. In addition, the vertical lines seem to point to the center photograph, drawing one's eye to it.

Pam Canavan, Clermont, Florida

Supplies: Striped paper (SEI); panoramic photo (Scrapbook Studio); letter stamps (Hero Arts); metal frame (Scrapworks); brown stamping ink; vellum; white cardstock; brads

Butterfly

Create the illusion of depth with shadows and repetition

After Sheila placed her focal-point photo and black border for this computer-generated layout, she selected and copied a section from the butterfly's wing. She created a black frame around it and then copied, rotated and placed the images in a vertical column. Through repetition of a smaller image, she created an interesting border and balanced the main image. Sheila then selected the shadow effect and applied it to her focal-point photo, title, butterflies and texture boxes. These shadows give the impression of texture, even though the elements are flat on the page. When placing shadows, Sheila says she tries to emulate the shadows in her focal photo.

Sheila McIntosh Dixon, Milton, Florida

Supplies: Image-editing software (Microsoft Digital Image Pro)

Dear Santa

Augment a layout with themed embellishments

Christmas cookie buttons are most appropriate for the holidays when they accent a photo featuring cookies for Santa. Stephanie also chose a charming Christmas ribbon and quilt patterned paper to conjure up images of home during the holidays. Several cardstock rectangles highlight words in Stephanie's journaling to add interest and break up the large block of text.

Stephanie Rarick, Elmendorf, Alaska

Supplies: Quilt patterned paper (K & Company); Christmas cookie buttons (Creative Imaginations); holly ribbon (Jo-Ann Fabrics); letter stickers (Foofala); date stamp (Making Memories); poem (by Patsy Gaut); gold glitter paper; evergreen, tan and red cardstocks; black stamping ink; letter tiles; chalk; black pen; foam tape

Holiday Mini Album

Enrich a theme album with unified design

Susan filled this album with full-page holiday photos opposite pages with plenty of white space, giving a clean, graphic look to each small spread. She used three fonts for the text throughout the book but combined them in unique ways to emphasize different points on each layout. Embellishments such as metal letters and fabric words add variety to the unified pages.

Susan Cyrus, Broken Arrow, Oklahoma

Supplies: Page pebbles, red swirl patterned paper, ribbon words and metal letters (Making Memories); image-editing software (Adobe Photoshop); jewels (Magic Scraps); rub-on letters (Creative Imaginations); white cardstock; brads; black pen

Fun
Feature analogous colors

Inspired by the reds and purples in her photos, Susan stuck to an analogous color scheme (colors that lie next to each other on the color wheel). Her mixture of light and dark colors cooperate for a balanced and fun look.

Susan Merrell, Starkville, Mississippi

Supplies: Color-blocked paper (Colorbök); rub-on letters (Making Memories); white and purple cardstocks

Mickey
Let curves in a photo inspire a similarly shaped design

Inspired by the shape of the askew mini-blinds in the photo, Elizabeth created curved lines above and below the photo using image-editing software. She employed text art features in her software to make the title and journaling follow the curves.

Elizabeth Lombardi, Yonkers, New York

Supplies: Image-editing software (Adobe Photoshop)

Happiness
Place a light-toned photo on a contrasting background

Robin used image-editing software to create a high-contrast page. The black background frames the light-valued photo and helps it pop off the page. Her orange and white title and journaling play off tones in the photo.

Robin Cecil, Odenton, Maryland

Supplies: Image-editing software (Microsoft Powerpoint)

Connor had an absolute
blast at his 2nd birthday
party! He grinned from
ear to ear the whole day.
Singing and dancing at
ABC Music for Kidz,
a guest list which included
Grannie and Papa, Aunt
Carol and Uncle Chad,
Danielle, Lauren, Melina,
Donovan and Cole and
their parents, and birthday
cake served on Elmo plates ...
What more could a 2-year-
old boy ask for?

If
you're
happy
and
you
know
it,
clap
your
hands!

two

Two

Unify a spread with punched shapes

Using several sizes of circle punches, Susan created colored circles and placed them randomly across both pages. One's eye follows the circles, thus unifying the spread. Her choice of primary colors coordinates with the bright photos and the children's party theme.

Susan Cyrus, Broken Arrow, Oklahoma

Supplies: Label maker (Dymo); circle punches (EK Success, Marvy); white, red, yellow, green and blue cardstocks; foam tape

While sitting at the depot
For our long-awaited bus
I noticed my son staring
Looking vaguely suspicious

Each member of the public
He did gravely scrutinize
Not one escaped unscathed from
The focus of his eyes

His thoughts remain unspoken
So I guess I'll never know
Just what he thought of all those
People, rushing to & fro

Public Scrutiny

Cross over a three-column grid with an enlarged photo

Shannon began with a basic three-column grid for this layout, but gave it a little kick by crossing over the columns. After she enlarged the digital photo of her son, she used a paint program to erase portions of the photo and a drawing program to render them transparent. This editing allowed her to create a strong focal point and left space for the whimsical poem she wrote about the day.

Shannon Freeman, Bellingham, Washington

Supplies: Image-editing software programs (Micrografx 6.0, Microsoft PhotoEditor, Microsoft Paint)

Everything

Emphasize photos through open space

Inspired by a book cover, Annie's page began with two colors of cardstock, each covering half of the page. A column of punched squares, highlighting some of her son's features, occupies the center of the page. Annie kept her embellishments to a minimum with a simple title and journaling block for a clean, open design. Her restraint with embellishments keeps one's attention focused on the column of snapshots.

Annie Wheatcraft, Frankfort, Kentucky

Supplies: Square punch (Marvy); letter stickers (EK Success); brown, tan and cream cardstocks

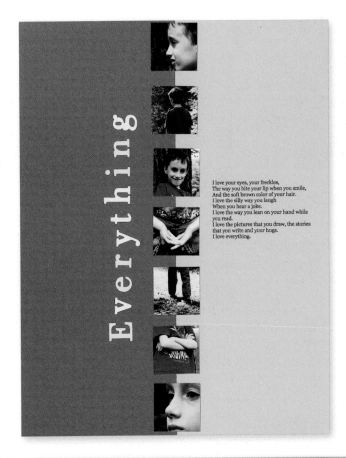

The Ocean Beckons Me

Blend symmetry and asymmetry

Sharon's horizontal paper strips along the top and bottom of both pages mirror each other—they are symmetrically balanced. Just as balanced though not mirror images of each other are her placement of photos and journaling on either page. The asymmetrically placed photos and journaling mix well with the symmetrical elements to create a spread that is well-balanced overall.

Sharon Whitehead, Vernon, British Columbia, Canada

Supplies: Letter page pebbles (Making Memories); circle cutter; tan, cream, powder blue, medium blue and blue cardstocks

Glossary of Design Terms

abstract shapes: simplified versions of natural shapes, such as symbols denoting restrooms

achromatic colors: a colorless scheme comprised of blacks, whites and grays

analogous colors: colors located next to each other on the color wheel

asymmetry: method of creating balance in which different objects with equal weight are distributed on a page

balance: equal distribution of weight on a page to create a pleasing arrangement of elements

bleeding: method of manipulating space in which elements extend over page edges

complementary colors: colors located directly across from one another on the color wheel

color wheel: artist's tool for matching and coordinating colors, arranged in a circular fashion

concept: a central idea or overall theme for a scrapbook page

contrast: variations and differences between light and dark colors

direction: the logical path that your eye should follow through a design

double complements: pairs of complementary colors used together

emphasis: the idea of making a certain element of a design stand out

focal point: the central place in which one's attention is drawn on a layout

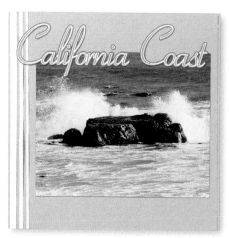

font: an assortment of type in one style

geometric shapes: structured shapes such as circle, square, rectangle, triangle, etc.

grid: the structured, underlying framework of a design

hierarchy: a system of organizing information in a design so that the most important elements are emphasized and noticed first

hue: another name for color

intensity: the brightness or dullness of a color

initial cap: The first letter of a title or paragraph, designed differently so that it stands out from other elements

key color: dominant color in a color scheme

monochromatic colors: various shades, tints or tones of one color

mood: the feeling created by choosing certain elements and colors to form a layout or design

natural shapes: figures occurring naturally such as the human body, plant and animal shapes

neutral colors: black, white, gray, brown and tan

optical weight: the appearance of heaviness or lightness in design, determined by positioning of elements

primary colors: red, yellow and blue; no other colors can be mixed together to create these colors

proportion: the comparative relationship between elements of a design with respect to size, amount and degree

repetition: including the same or similar elements more than once in a layout to create rhythm

rhythm: creating the illusion of movement or motion in a design

rule of thirds: concept that divides a space into nine equal sections with vertical and horizontal lines; for a pleasing composition, your subject should fall on or near any of the points where the lines intersect

sans serif: a type style without finishing lines on the ends of letters

secondary colors: purple, green and orange; colors derived by combining primaries (red + blue = purple, yellow + blue = green, yellow + red = orange)

serif: a type style with tiny lines that finish off the ends of each letter

shade: color with black added

space: the distance or area between or around page elements

split complements: a color that is paired with the two colors located on either side of its complement

spread: a layout consisting of two pages that flow together

symmetry: when one side of a layout is the mirror image of the other and contains the same number of elements

tactile texture: dimension that can be felt

tertiary colors: a primary color mixed with a secondary color

tint: color with white added

tone: color with gray added

triadic complements: three colors equally spaced from each other on the color wheel; their placement on the wheel forms a triangle

unity: when all elements look like they belong together

value: lightness or darkness of a color

visual texture: patterns that appear dimensional to the eye but are actually flat

z-flow: method of arranging page elements so the eye flows across the page in a "z" shape, allowing one to read the message of the page clearly

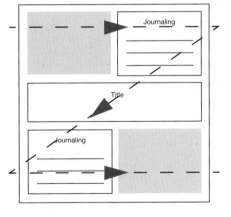

Additional credits

Charm de Village (p. 6)

Michele Gerbrandt's photos taken in France were accented with conceptual embellishments that fit the architecture theme. A tin background was painted to match the gate and stone church in the photos. Archircture-style premade embellishments further complement the design.

Supplies: Tin sheet (Artistic Expressions); acrylic paints (Delta); metallic rub-ons (Craf-T); premade architecture embellishments (EK Success); vellum; teal and gray cardstocks; clear embossing powder

Rule of Thirds (p. 42)

Photo by Jackie Raines, Canton, Michigan

Sources

The following companies manufacture products showcased on scrapbook pages within this book. Please check your local retailers to find these materials. We have made every attempt to properly credit the items mentioned in this book and apologize to those we may have missed.

7 Gypsies
(800) 588-6707
www.7gypsies.com

A Stamp In The Hand Co.
(310) 884-9700
www.astampinthehand.com

Adobe
www.adobe.com

All My Memories
(888) 553-1998
www.allmymemories.com

All Night Media (see Plaid Enterprises)

American Art Clay Company (AMACO)
(800) 374-1600
www.amaco.com

American Crafts
(800) 879-5185
www.americancrafts.com

American Tag Company
(800) 223-3956
www.americantag.net

Amscan, Inc.
(800) 444-8887
www.amscan.com

Anna Griffin, Inc (wholesale only)
(888) 817-8170
www.annagriffin.com

Artistic Expressions
(219) 764-5158
www.artisticexpressionsinc.com

Artistic Scrapper
(818) 786-8304
www.artisticscrapper.com

Autumn Leaves (wholesale only)
(800) 588-6707
www.autumnleaves.com

Avery Dennison Corporation
(800) G0-AVERY
www.avery.com

Bazzill Basics Paper
(480) 558-8557
www.bazzillbasics.com

Bisous
(905) 502-7209
www.bisous.biz

Blue Moon Beads
(800) 377-6715
www.bluemoonbeads.com

Blumenthal Lansing
(201) 935-6220
www.buttonsplus.com

Bo-Bunny Press
(801) 771-0481
www.bobunny.com

Books By Hand
(505) 255-3534

Broderbund Software
www.broderbund.com

Bulldog Hardware—no contact info available

Canson, Inc.®
(800) 628-9283
www.canson-us.com

Carolee's Creations®
(435) 563-1100
www.ccpaper.com

Chatterbox, Inc.
(208) 939-9133
www.chatterboxinc.com

Chronicle Books
(800) 722-6656
www.chroniclebooks.com

Clearsnap, Inc.
(800) 448-4862
www.clearsnap.com

Close To My Heart®
(888) 655-6552
www.closetomyheart.com

Club Scrap™
(888) 634-9100
www.clubscrap.com

Colorbök™, Inc. (wholesale only)
(800) 366-4660
www.colorbok.com

Cousin Corporation of America, CCA
(800) 366-2687
www.cousin.com

Craf-T Products
(507) 235-3996
www.craf-tproducts.com

Crafter's Workshop, The
(877) CRAFTER
www.thecraftersworkshop.com

Creative Block, The/Stampers Anonymous
(888) 326-0012
www.stampersanonymous.com

Creative Imaginations (wholesale only)
(800) 942-6487
www.cigift.com

Creative Impressions
(719) 596-4860
www.creativeimpressions.com

Creative Memories®
(800) 468-9335
www.creativememories.com

Creative Papers Online Handmade Paper
(800) PAPER-40
www.handmade-paper.us

Cropper Hopper™/Advantus Corporation (wholesale only)
(800) 826-8806
www.cropperhopper.com

C-Thru® Ruler Company, The (wholesale only)
(800) 243-8419
www.cthruruler.com

Daisy D's Paper Company
(888) 601-8955
www.daisydspaper.com

Darice, Inc.
(800) 321-1494
www.darice.com

DecoArt™, Inc.
(800) 367-3047
www.decoart.com

Delta Technical Coatings, Inc.
(800) 423-4135
www.deltacrafts.com

Deluxe Designs
(480) 497-9005
www.deluxecuts.com

Design Originals
(800) 877-7820
www.d-originals.com

DieCuts with a View™
(801) 224-6766
www.diecutswithaview.com

DMD Industries, Inc. (wholesale only)
(800) 805-9890
www.dmdind.com

Dolphin Enterprises
(801) 495-7234
www.protect-a-page.com

Doodlebug Design Inc.
(801) 952-0555
www.doodlebugdesigninc.com

Dymo
www.dymo.com

Educational Insights
(800) 995-4436
www.edin.com

EK Success™, Ltd. (wholesale only)
(800) 524-1349
www.eksuccess.com

Emagination Crafts, Inc. (wholesale only)
(630) 833-9521
www.emaginationcrafts.com

Family Treasures, Inc.®
www.familytreasures.com

Fiber Scraps™
(215) 230-4905
www.fiberscraps.com

Fibers By The Yard™
(405) 364-8066
www.fibersbytheyard.com

Fibre-Craft®
www.fibrecraft.com

Fiskars, Inc. (wholesale only)
(715) 842-2091
www.fiskars.com

Foofala
(402) 330-3208
www.foofala.com

Frances Meyer, Inc.®
(800) 372-6237
www.francesmeyer.com

Generations
(800) 905-1888
www.Generationsnow.com

Got Memories—no contact info available

Graphic Products Corp.
(800) 323-1660
www.grafixarts.com

Graphic Products Corporation
(800) 323-1660
www.gpcpapers.com

Halcraft USA, Inc.
(212) 376-1580
www.halcraft.com

Happy Hammer, The
(303) 690-3883
www.thehappyhammer.com

Hasbro®
www.hasbro.com

Heart & Home, Inc./Melissa Frances
(905) 686-9031
www.melissafrances.com

Herma—no contact info available

Hero Arts® Rubber Stamps, Inc. (wholesale only)
(800) 822-4376
www.heroarts.com

Hewlett-Packard Company
(650) 857-1501
www.hp.com

Hillcreek Designs
(619) 562-5799
www.hillcreekdesigns.com

Hirschberg Schutz & Co., Inc.
(800) 221-8640

Hobby Lobby Stores, Inc.
www.hobbylobby.com

Hot Off The Press, Inc.
(800) 227-9595
www.paperpizazz.com

Jesse James & Co., Inc.
(610) 435-0201
www.jessejamesbutton.com

JewelCraft LLC
(201) 223-0804
www.jewelcraft.biz

Jo-Ann Fabrics & Crafts
(888) 739-4120
www.joann.com

JudiKins
(310) 515-1115
www.judikins.com

Junkitz™
(732) 792-1180
www.junkitz.com

K & Company
(888) 244-2083
www.kandcompany.com

K & S® Metals/K & S® Engineering
(773) 586-8503
www.ksmetals.com

Kangaroo & Joey®, Inc.
(800) 646-8065
www.kangarooandjoey.com

Karen Foster Design™ (wholesale only)
(801) 451-9779
www.karenfosterdesign.com

KI Memories
www.kimemories.com

Krylon
(216) 566-2000
www.krylon.com

La Pluma, Inc.
(615) 273-7367
www.debrabeagle.com

Lasting Impressions for Paper, Inc.
(801) 298-1979
www.lastingimpressions.com

Laura's Crafts—no contact info
available

Li'l Davis Designs
(949) 838-0344
www.lildavisdesigns.com

Limited Edition Rubber Stamps
(650) 594-4242
www.LimitedEditionRS.com

Lion Brand Yarn Company
www.lionbrand.com

Liquitex® Artist Materials
(888) 4-ACRYLIC
www.liquitex.com

Magenta Rubber Stamps
(wholesale only)
(800) 565-5254
www.magentarubberstamps.com

Magic Mesh™
(651) 345-6374
www.magicmesh.com

Magic Scraps™
(972) 238-1838
www.magicscraps.com

Making Memories
(800) 286-5263
www.makingmemories.com

Marvy® Uchida (wholesale only)
(800) 541-5877
www.uchida.com

McGill Inc.
(800) 982-9884
www.mcgillinc.com

me & my BiG ideas® (wholesale only)
(949) 583-2065
www.meandmybigideas.com

Microsoft Corporation
www.microsoft.com

MOD (my own design)
(303) 641-8680
www.mod-myowndesign.com

Mrs. Grossman's Paper Co.
(wholesale only)
(800) 429-4549
www.mrsgrossmans.com

Mustard Moon™
(408) 229-8542
www.mustardmoon.com

My Mind's Eye™, Inc.
(801) 298-3709
www.frame-ups.com

National Cardstock
(866) 452-7120
www.nationalcardstock.com

NRN Designs
(800) 421-6958
www.nrndesigns.com

Office Depot
www.officedepot.com

Office Max
www.officemax.com

Offray
www.offray.com

On The Surface
(847) 675-2520

Paper Adventures® (wholesale only)
(800) 727-0699
www.paperadventures.com

Paper Company™, The
(800) 426-8989
www.anwcrestwood.com

Paper Fever, Inc.
(801) 412-0495
www.paperfever.com

Paper Loft, The
(801) 254-1961
www.paperloft.com

Paper Patch, The
(800) 397-2737
www.paperpatch.com

Pebbles, Inc.
(800) 438-8153
www.pebblesinc.com

Pepperell Braiding Company
(800) 343-8114
www.pepperell.com

Pixie Press
(888) 834-2883
www.pixiepress.com

Plaid Enterprises, Inc.
(800) 842-4197
www.plaidonline.com

Postmodern Design
(405) 321-3176
www.stampdiva.com

PrintWorks
(800) 854-6558
www.printworkscollection.com

Provo Craft® (wholesale only)
(888) 577-3545
www.provocraft.com

Prym-Dritz Corporation
www.dritz.com

PSX Design™
(800) 782-6748
www.psxdesign.com

Punch Bunch, The
(254) 791-4209
www.thepunchbunch.com

Queen & Co./The Eyelet Queen
(858) 485-5132
www.eyeletqueen.com

QuickKutz®
(888) 702-1146
www.quickkutz.com

Robin's Nest Press, The
(435) 789-5387

Rockler—no contact info available

Rubber Stampede
(800) 423-4135
www.rubberstampede.com

Rusty Pickle
(801) 272-2280
www.rustypickle.com

Sandylion Sticker Designs
(800) 387-4215
www.sandylion.com

Scrapbook Studio—no contact info
available

Scrapbook Wizard™, The
(435) 752-7555
www.scrapbookwizard.com

Scrap Ease®
(800) 272-3874
www.whatsnewltd.com

Scrap Pagerz™
(435) 645-0696
www.scrappagerz.com

Scrapworks, LLC
(801) 363-1010
www.scrapworks.com

Scrapyard 329
(775) 829-1118
www.scrapyard329.com

SEI, Inc.
(800) 333-3279
www.shopsei.com

Sizzix
(866) 742-4447
www.sizzix.com

Sports Solution
(303) 466-4220

S.R.M. Press, Inc.
(800) 323-9589
www.srmpress.com

Stampabilities®
(800) 888-0321
www.stampabilities.com

Stampendous®/Mark Enterprises
(800) 869-0474
www.stampendous.com

Stampington & Company
(877) STAMPER
www.stampington.com

Stampin' Up!®
(800) 782-6787
www.stampinup.com

Sticker Studio™
(208) 322-2465
www.stickerstudio.com

Sweetwater
(800) 359-3094
www.sweetwaterscrapbook.com

Target
www.target.com

Treehouse Designs
(877) 372-1109
www.treehouse-designs.com

Tsukineko®, Inc.
(800) 769-6633
www.tsukineko.com

Tumblebeasts LLC
(505) 323-5554
www.tumblebeasts.com

Wal-Mart Stores, Inc.
(800) WALMART
www.walmart.com

Westrim® Crafts
(800) 727-2727
www.westrimcrafts.com

Wordsworth
(719) 282-3495
www.wordsworthstamps.com

Index